MY FAVO...

LIFE-CHANGING STORIES

JOE L. WHEELER

Pacific Press®
Publishing Association

Nampa, Idaho | Oshawa, Ontario, Canada
www.pacificpress.com

Cover design by Gerald Lee Monks
Cover design resources from Marcus Mashburn
Inside design by Aaron Troia

The author assumes full responsibility for the accuracy
of all facts and quotations as cited in this book.

Scripture quotations marked KJV are from the King
James Version.

Scripture quotations marked NET are from the NET
Bible® copyright © 1996–2016 by Biblical Studies
Press, LLC. All rights reserved.

Scripture quotations marked NLT are taken from the
Holy Bible, New Living Translation, copyright © 1996,
2004, 2007, 2013, 2015 by Tyndale House Foundation. Used by permission of Tyndale House Publishers,
Inc., Carol Stream, Illinois 60188. All rights reserved.

You can obtain additional copies of this book by
calling toll-free 1-800-765-6955 or by visiting
http://www.adventistbookcenter.com.

Library of Congress Cataloging-in-Publication Data
Names: Wheeler, Joe L., 1936- compiler.
Title: My favorite life-changing stories /
    [compiled by] Joe L. Wheeler.
Description: Nampa : Pacific Press Publishing, 2017.
Identifiers: LCCN 2016046299 |
    ISBN 9780816361977 (pbk.)
Subjects: LCSH: Encouragement—Religious aspects
    —Christianity. | Inspiration—Religious aspects
    —Christianity.
Classification: LCC BV4647.E53 M9 2017 | DDC
    242—dc23 LC record available at https://lccn.loc
    .gov/2016046299

December 2016

DEDICATION

As I look back through the quarter of a century of our ministry, and think of all the men and women who have made our story anthologies possible, foremost among them are all those hundreds of people who have sent us copies of their favorite stories. But even among those, there are certain individuals who stand out. These are the kindred spirits who have cherished stories that touch the heart all the days of their lives. And serendipitously for us, a number of them (when they reach the age when they aren't using their story collections much anymore) think of us, and brighten our lives by bequeathing their collections to us. Knowing what a sacrifice on their part such gifting means to them, I never take such heartfelt gifts for granted.

Thus it is, as I write the dedication for our ninety-fifth book (eightieth story anthology), I noticed that one of these stories, "Out of Focus," author unknown, came to us as part of a story collection a certain individual had spent a lifetime assembling. In gratitude for her sacrifice, and in gratitude to all those others who have sent us stories over the years, it is my great privilege to dedicate *My Favorite Life-Changing Stories* to

VALEETAH MOTSCHIEDLER
of Riverside, California

CONTENTS

EPILOGUE

O ne of the most frustrating aspects of life is that there are so many choices along the way: we are constantly having to choose one option, one road, instead of the other. Frost implies that choices are not necessarily between good and bad, but rather between two goods of roughly equal value. But, oh, how he wishes he could explore both—or at least come back again sometime. But he sighs,

"Yet knowing how way leads on to way,
I doubted if I should ever come back."

THE DIVERGING ROADS OF OUR LIVES
Joseph Leininger Wheeler

Robert Frost's most famous poem begins with these words:

"Two roads diverged in a yellow wood."
—*"The Road Not Taken"*

Yet, we also know that God knows the end from the beginning: in His omniscience, even allowing for our free-choice, He somehow knows which one we'll choose. Or as Elizabeth Goudge put it in her powerful book, *Pilgrim's Inn*: "We can liken life to a series of deaths and rebirths, each predestined, so that when you reached it you recognized it as something that had been waiting for you, and yet each at the same time the result of a matter of choice, so that you came to it with a joy or pain of your own making, a paradox whose mystery baffles the mind but whose truth the heart recognizes."

But some of these divergences turn out to be far more significant than what we at first assume they'll be. I often take daily walks when we visit our son Greg in Fort Lauderdale. What never ceases to amaze me is how easy it is, when you're not familiar with a city, to lose your bearings, ending up miles from where you thought you were.

Just so, one never knows where an unknown diverging road will take you. In life, rarely do we realize in the moment which divergence will be major and which will be but a blip in our life's journey.

Which leads us to a fascinating literary word, *epiphany*. According to *Merriam-Webster*, other than references to January 6 and the appearance or manifestation of a divine being, it can be categorized as:

- A usually sudden manifestation or perception of the essential nature or meaning of something.

- An intuitive grasp of reality through something (as an event) usually simple and striking.

- An illuminating discovery, realization, or disclosure.

- A revealing scene or moment.

All of these you will discover in our stories. Throughout my adult lifetime, I've been searching for, and occasionally finding, stories having to do with pivotal moments, experiences, or days in a given person's life. And now, what a joy to gather together some of the most emotive, inspirational, powerful ones into one collection.

The beauty of such stories is that we can learn from the mistakes of others rather than making them ourselves. I have drawn from a time period spanning close to 150 years, which results in a much more significant breadth and depth of experience than would be true of a collection of all contemporary stories.

As to specific story attributions, most of the authors will be unfamiliar to you. Some, such as Frederick Hall, Margaret Sangster, Will Carleton, and Arthur Gordon, you're likely to already know and cherish. Sadly, many remain unknown. Do let me know if you recognize the authorship of any of the stories so we can update those attributions in future printings.

Coda

I would love to hear from you, as to your reaction to these stories. You may even be able to track down authors to old stories or even descendants to those authors. You may reach me at:

> Joe L. Wheeler, PhD
> PO Box 1246
> Conifer, CO 80433

A *charismatic untried young President—and a bald-headed, shoe-pounding dictator: the two most powerful men in the world were playing a nuclear game of chicken. Which one of them would push the nuclear button first?*

American school children everywhere were being led by their teachers in terrifying bomb drills. The world teetered on the edge of nuclear catastrophe. Was this the end of the world as we knew it? The showdown had to do with an island called Cuba, about ninety miles off the Florida coast. How well I remember Kennedy's ragged voice as he announced to the American people that the United States was quarantining Cuba and warning Russia that it must leave.

Little did Jerome Hines, the Metropolitan Opera basso acclaimed as one of the operatic immortals of the twentieth century, know that his greatest performance was only hours way. But he was prepared—because he'd already faced a life-changing showdown between his pride and his God. Had his pride won, chances are he wouldn't have been in Moscow that fateful evening.

PROLOGUE

A VOICE FOR GOD
Jerome Hines

It was 3:00 A.M., Moscow time, October 23, 1962, when President Kennedy went on the air to announce the American quarantine of Cuba. My wife, Lucia, and I were asleep in Moscow's Metropole Hotel. Two blocks away lights were ablaze in the Kremlin.

For me it was the last day of a five-week singing tour of the Soviet Union. A final performance of *Boris Godunov* was booked for that evening at the Bolshoi Theater.

At breakfast, Bill Jones, a friend and traveling companion, told us that he had heard a rumor about a new crisis between Russia and America. Four hours later we had lunch with Foy Kohler, the American ambassador. He confirmed to us officially that the United States had established a quarantine of Cuba.

Immediately, we wondered what effect all this would have on our evening performance of *Boris*. Would there be demonstrations against Americans? The ambassador, however, had reassuring words, "The Russian people have not been told about the crisis."

The rest of the day was tension-filled. Back at the hotel, we packed, made a few phone calls, and then tried to rest. About 3 P.M., I left the hotel for the half hour's walk I take before each performance.

As I walked past the Kremlin, past St. Basil's Cathedral, I was thinking about the many occasions in my life when I had needed God—but, how the steady flow of His guidance had always been dependent on my obedience. . . .

Ten years before, in 1952, I had first learned to listen for His Help. At that time there was a great conflict going on in my life. On one hand, I did not want God interfering in my life, upsetting my plans and my desires. On the other, I found myself pulled strongly toward Him.

Meanwhile, it was in this year of 1952 that a performance of *Boris Godunov* was scheduled by the Metropolitan Opera. More than anything else I wanted to play the role of Boris. I felt that I was ready for it. The opera manager did not agree. We argued, and I threatened to quit.

But in the end, I received the role. When self-doubt took over, however, it became a hollow victory. For now that I had won this great responsibility, I was obsessed by the fear of failure. And a failure in this assignment could ruin my career. In desperation I conceived an idea for a publicity stunt. Near the end of the opera Boris, dying, plunges down the stairs. With this fall I would feign a back injury.

"Opera star injured in fall." I could see the headlines. What a boost all this publicity would be to my career.

That night in a hotel room in New York, I wrestled with the still small voice of God in my heart.

Is it honest to fake an injury?

"Honesty hasn't anything to do with it," I countered. "What would You have me do?"

Would you be willing to give up the publicity stunt?

"No!" was my instant reaction.

For long agonizing moments I argued with myself. Finally, I realized that either I had to surrender myself to God or separate myself completely from Him.

"All right," I said. "I'll do what You tell me. I want You before all else in my life."

Then came the inner instruction: *open the Bible and there will be your answer.*

When I had checked into the room I noticed a Gideon Bible on top of the dresser. Obeying the order, I got out of bed, opened the Bible, and my eyes fell upon these words:

"Who shall ascend into the hill of the Lord? . . . He that hath clean hands, and a pure heart; who hath not lifted up his soul unto vanity, nor sworn deceitfully" (Psalm 24:3, 4, KJV).

Give up your silly, egocentric publicity scheme and get on with your work. How much clearer can guidance be!

The next morning I began to concentrate on the score. So absorbed did I become with the character of Boris that I wrote a psychoanalysis of him which was later published. The total result was that when I did sing *Boris Godunov* at the Met [Mr. Hines was the first American-born basso to perform the role of Boris], newspaper reviews could not have been more generous.

This experience of obedience to God revolutionized not only my career but also my entire life. And yet spiritual growth was so often blocked by my ego. Time after time I would charge ahead on my own steam, only to fall on my face. On each occasion, I would tell myself once and for all to get out of my own way and let God run my life.

Then came the challenge of a lifetime! An opportunity to sing *Boris Godunov* in Russian with the Bolshoi Opera Company in Moscow.

The trip was planned to begin with an August, 1962, tour of Argentina and then a flight from Buenos Aires to Moscow. A week before Lucia and I were to leave, a revolution threatened in Argentina. My agent insisted that we cancel the South American part of the tour, but I hesitated to do this.

We were vacationing at the time near Seaside Park, New Jersey. One moonlit night several days later I felt impelled to go out for a walk. It was almost as if God wanted to tell me something about the trip and could do so best out under His skies.

Now I realize that guidance comes to different people in different ways. Some people obtain it through meditation and Bible reading. To others it arrives at odd moments in the form of quiet mental nudges.

There are times, to be sure, when I want direction, but all I can hear are my own thoughts clamoring for control. Yet I know it is not real guidance when I keep asking over and over, "Now, God, is this what I am supposed to do?" For if God is trying to tell me something, I feel it so strongly that there is no doubt.

On this night I received instructions so clear that I hardly could believe them:

The important thing for you to do is obey Me. For the next two months there will be such a circle of protection around you that Satan cannot touch you. Do your task joyfully. Believe always and have faith, for I am with you every step of the way.

Six days later Lucia and I were on our way to Argentina. By the time we arrived, the situation had quieted down and all performances went smoothly. Our stay was delightful.

On September 19, we flew out of Buenos Aires for Moscow. On the twentieth riots broke out in Argentina, jets were bombing Buenos Aires, and the airport was closed down immediately. We had gotten out on one of the last planes. The timing of all this was so remarkable that it further strengthened my conviction that I must obey . . . obey . . . obey.

Lucia and I felt that our trip to Russia involved much more than the fulfillment of my longtime dream of being the first American-born basso to do *Boris* in Russian at the Bolshoi. Here was an opportunity to take a stand for Christ in various ways before the Russian people.

How can you do this in an atheistic country? We had some definite ideas. But our witness would not amount to anything unless my performance of *Boris* was effective.

That is why we both were so upset by what

happened to me when we arrived in Moscow. I came down with a throat infection three days before my opening performance of *Boris* at the Bolshoi on Sunday, September 23. The Russian doctor said that I could not sing. I took the pills he gave me and went to bed.

But the big question was not what the Russian doctor ordered but what God wanted. I opened my Bible and read this passage:

"So you, my [son], be strong in the grace that is in Christ Jesus. . . . Take your share of suffering as a good soldier of Christ Jesus" (2 Timothy 2:1, 3, NET).

A soldier is under orders. He must obey if the mission is to be accomplished. I knew then that nothing was to be canceled. I was to go ahead despite the doctor's orders, trusting God to provide the voice and the strength.

But Sunday night when I arrived at the theater, my throat still was a question mark. And by the last act, I had little voice left.

Before the last curtain I went behind some scenery in the wings to wrestle this crisis through in prayer. *If my voice fails*, I thought, *the whole Russian trip is finished.* Had I mistaken my guidance? Or was my faith being tested to the limit?

In my extremity, I saw clearly that I was to go on stage in God's strength—not mine. And at the moment I needed it, the promised help came. My tension vanished. An energy from beyond myself revitalized me. My voice was clear, strong.

Later, Lucia and our associates told me that this was the finest act of *Boris* I had ever performed.

In the weeks that followed, the inflow of energy and help continued. Facing an impossible schedule of twelve performances and twelve rehearsals in a thirty-day tour of Russian cities, I felt the Holy Spirit inside me, guiding me, giving me strength and courage.

There were ways to show our faith in God too. Lucia and I long had made it a practice to say a quiet blessing in public restaurants before eating; we did this throughout Russia. To the Russian people assigned to help us during the tour, we found occasions to talk about Jesus Christ. We attended church services when possible and invited our Russian contacts to go with us.

During one performance in Leningrad the chorus applauded me backstage. Impulsively I told them in Russian, "Give God the credit, not me." For a moment there was stunned silence—then louder applause than before. . . .

And now we were down to the last day, the final *Boris* back in Moscow with the threat of nuclear war over us all.

At 6:15 P.M. I was in my dressing room and nearly finished with my makeup. Curtain time at the Bolshoi is 6:30 P.M. Suddenly there were excited voices outside and the stage director burst in.

"Khrushchev's here."

Bill Jones and I stared at each other. Two weeks before we had both felt an odd premonition that this last *Boris* at the Bolshoi would be surrounded by unusual circumstances. How right we had been!

The first act went well. Between acts Lucia and our interpreter rushed backstage. "Jerry," she said, "are you trying to start an international incident? Khrushchev led a standing ovation for you. But you didn't acknowledge it."

"I didn't see him."

"He's in the right hand box."

I calmed them down and promised them I would find a way to acknowledge him.

The opera is set in czarist times at the turn of the century. Boris has committed murder to gain the throne. In the final scene, guilt-ridden, insane, and dying, he cries out to God, "Forgive me," and then dies.

I saw a chance to inject a note of Christian hope, to show that Boris, after asking forgiveness, finds salvation and peace through Jesus Christ. So, after the words "forgive me," with radiant uplifted head as his plea is answered, Boris—as I interpreted him—cries gratefully "Oh, my God."

At previous *Boris* performances in Moscow, Kiev, and Tbilisi, the Russians had responded to this additional emphasis with enthusiasm. How would Khrushchev, an avowed atheist, feel about it?

Everything built up perfectly to this climax. When the final scene came, Boris weakly then exultantly found repentance and, dying, plunged down the stairs.

Instead of waiting for the postlude before applauding, as is customary, this audience broke all precedent by rising at this point. Pounding his hands together in front of them all was a familiar bald-headed figure.

I walked over in front of Premier Khrushchev's box and bowed.

It was a day later when I realized the significance of Khrushchev's presence at the Bolshoi that night. Papers throughout the world reported that by paying a tribute to an American singer, he was indicating the future conciliatory role his government would follow in the Cuban crisis.

If this is true and God was able to use me in this emergency, I am very grateful. For I know that God wants to reach the Russian people. He does have a plan to bring Christ into our hearts. But that plan needs obedient disciples. This means me—and you.

SECTION ONE

"Honor your father and mother.
Then you will live a long, full life in the land
the Lord your God is giving you."
—Exodus 20:12, NLT

One of the most cherished stories penned during the last eighty years is this one, written during the Great Depression of the 1930s. The issue is this: If you are all but destitute, can you still give? The story confirms what I have long thought: It isn't the monetary value of a gift that means the most, it is the heart behind the gift.

THE GOLDEN MOMENT

Author Unknown

He was a very old, very appealing little man, and he stood hesitatingly upon the corner of two streets, both congested with traffic, and looked wistfully across to the corner opposite. Once he started forward toward the curb, but, shaking his head decidedly, he drew back and glanced up and down the street.

Elizabeth was standing perhaps twenty feet away from him, waiting for her car, and it was not until she saw it coming and stepped forth to signal it, that she noticed the undecided figure wavering upon the edge of the walk. She signaled the car to go on, and impulsively ran back to the little old man's side.

"Let me help you across," she said.

His face lighted up, his cheeks glowed rosily, and his eyes shone as he clung to her strong young arm, and was ferried through the stream of traffic safely to the other side.

"There!" Elizabeth said, and smiled her brightest smile.

"Bless you, child! But," self-reproachfully,

"I made you miss your car."

"It doesn't matter in the least."

"I'm very glad of that," he said, simply. "You've given me my golden moment, child—with your help and your smile."

"Your golden moment?" Elizabeth was frankly puzzled.

He nodded. "Yes, my golden moment," he answered. "You know there is one golden moment in every hour for everyone—if we only look for it."

"Is there?" Elizabeth stammered. "I didn't know it."

"No?" It was the old man's turn to look surprised. "Why, of course there is, my dear. Look out for your golden moments, and you will see."

He smiled, lifting his hat and disclosing his thin white curly hair, and was gone down the street. Elizabeth stood a moment at the corner, letting another homeward-bound car pass.

"A golden moment in every hour!" she mused. "That dear old man—perhaps there is, for him. But someone doesn't do something nice for me every hour; I'm sure of that. No, nor for any of us. I know Mother doesn't have a golden moment in every hour."

As she spoke, her eyes rested on the window of a florist's shop beside her. One window was filled with bunches of purple violets and maidenhair fern. Elizabeth's eyes lighted up as she looked at the flowers. Violets were her own as well as her mother's favorite flowers.

"If I only had a bunch of them to take to Mother," she said wistfully, peering into her purse, and closing it with a sigh. She had nothing but carfare—one bright silver dime. And her car was coming.

She stepped to the edge of the curb, then halted. Her mind skipped nimbly over the blocks between herself and home. There were a great many of them.

"But I often walked farther before we came to the city," Elizabeth said. "I believe I'll do it!"

Turning her back on the approaching car, she hurried into the shop with its perfumed interior, and came out with the violets and their fringe of maidenhair wrapped in green oiled paper. Holding them carefully, she turned toward home.

"How pleased Mother will be! No one has brought her flowers in—I don't know how long. I know she'll be pleased."

And Mrs. Horton *was* pleased. Her face flushed with surprise and delight when she carefully opened the package, and the violets were revealed.

"And you walked home that I might have them!" she cried, brokenly. "O Elizabeth!"

"That's all right, Mother," Elizabeth said briskly. "I enjoyed the walk. I don't believe I get enough exercise anyway. Why, Mother—Mother—you are crying!"

Mrs. Horton hid her face in the flowers for a moment. "Don't mind me, dear," she said, a little quaveringly. "It's just because I've been such a dreadful and ungrateful mother. I'm ashamed to admit it, but I was nearly ready to give up this evening. The children have been so restless today, and everything has gone wrong. I thought I was a failure as a mother, and I couldn't stand it. Then you came with your violets—and, O, I can't tell you any more!" She buried her head upon Elizabeth's shoulder and sobbed a little, then went with shining face to put the violets in water.

"She has her golden moment—when she needs it so much," Elizabeth whispered to herself as she removed her coat and hat. "Yes, who is it?" she called, in response to a timid rap on the door.

"It's Teddy," said a disconsolate little voice as the door opened. "I've got a story here, but there wasn't anyone to read it to me. I don't suppose you have the time?"

Elizabeth hesitated a moment. She did so

want to work a little on her new frock. But what of Teddy's golden moments—had he had many during the day? She looked at his wistful and questioning little face, and gathered him into her arms.

"Where is the story?" she demanded. "Let's not let it go unread another instant. And after I've read it, we'll see if you can learn to read just a tiny bit."

She read the story, and patiently taught him the sounds of several letters to remember until the following evening, when she would read him another story and teach him a few more letters. Then they went down to supper.

Mr. Horton sat in the light, looking old and careworn. Elizabeth threw her arms around his neck, holding his cheek against her own. "Dear old Daddy," she said, "he works so hard for us all. I wish you didn't have to work so hard, Father."

His eyes lighted up, and the tired lines seemed magically erased. "You work pretty steady yourself, little daughter," he said. "It isn't the work that a person minds so much—it's just the feeling a man gets sometimes that maybe no one cares. It lifts his burdens to

have a couple of arms around his neck like—" He choked, and broke off. Elizabeth kissed him, and went slowly to her chair.

After supper when she had praised Harvey until his boyish cheeks glowed redly, for some point wherein he deserved praise, and made Betty, the real helper of her mother, the sweeping cap of pink-and-white lawn which she had wanted for so long, she told them about the old man and his golden moment.

"You've given each of us at least one of pure eighteen-carat gold," her father said, "but I don't see where you come in. You have not had a single one."

Elizabeth stared breathlessly for a moment. "Why—yes—I have," she cried. "Why it seems as if they have all been golden! I believe you can't give a golden moment without getting one in return. I've had more than my share—more than the rest of you."

Her father looked at her shining face. "It sounds like a good investment," he remarked. "Suppose we all try to see if it works with us, too. I believe we shall be a happier family if we do."

"I know we shall!" Elizabeth cried.

*T*he older I get the more convinced I become that there are no "little things" in life. Just as is true with this story, I, too, have sometimes come perilously close to "running away" from responsibilities, from those who depend upon me, those who believe in me. Almost, it sometimes seems to me, it's like my guardian angel occasionally has to step in to save me from myself.

ABSENT WITH LEAVE

Frederick Hall

This story Captain Boyd told me in France in wartime. Lefty Smith, a private in his company and an excellent fighting man, had to our sorrow gone AWOL, and we were saying to one another—what is known to every man who has been long with an army—that a deserter is often far more to be pitied than blamed, for war is at times
sickening, at times extremely monotonous. "Why," exclaimed the captain, "I think a flat tire was all that kept me from deserting once. Instead I went AWL—absent *with* leave."

Then he told me this story.

The smell of the new-cut hay would have brought a pang of homesickness to Capt. James Boyd of the Marines, but to Jimmy Boyd, in patched blue overalls, climbing the ladder to the haymow of the cow barn at the home farm on Blue River, it brought a feeling of utter disgust. Hadn't he helped cut that hay, helped load it, helped bring it in from the field, and helped pack it away there? The tan of those haying days was still on his cheeks, the horny coating of his palms came in part from blisters, his muscles still ached as he remembered the weight of the heavy pitchfork. To one who has recently worked in the hayfield the smell of new-mown hay is not what it is to the poet.

Jimmy reached the hayloft, listened, and peered down the shaft up which he had climbed. Save for the buzzing of a scouting wasp, fighting through cobweb entanglements, there was no sound. He was alone. Suddenly, like a gopher, he ducked down a burrow. Its end was against the barn wall, and cracks and a knothole let in enough of the mid-afternoon sunlight so he could dimly discern his cramped surroundings. He groped a moment, elbow-deep in the hay, and drew forth a leather-hinged box of light pine. One vigorous kick would have demolished it; nevertheless it was closed with a clasp and a padlock whose key hung from a string round his neck. Inside were a .22-caliber revolver, two boxes of cartridges, a felt hat of rakish appearance, a jackknife with its two blades sharpened to a razor edge, a sort of brown canvas knapsack, and a leather bag that gathered with a string, and contained three dollars and eighty-eight cents, all in coins, besides a few minor treasures. Jim put the hat on, took out a souvenir pocket mirror presented by the Eltonville Cash Department Store and, squirming about to get just the right light, contemplated his impressive reflection. He opened the knife and felt the sharpness of its blades; he licked the back of his hand, drew the blade across it and noted with satisfaction how perfectly the soft fuzz was shaved away. He picked up the revolver, raised the hammer and lowered it, took out the chamber, and filled it with cartridges and then removed them; with an oily rag he polished it, giving particular attention to a spot upon which a drop of perspiration had fallen—it was suffocatingly hot in his hay cavern. He opened the knapsack slowly, lovingly—and then a voice broke in on his preoccupation:

"Jim! O Jim!"

His father was calling from the orchard. Jim hesitated. If he stayed where he was, his father might think he was out of hearing, in the wood lot or perhaps in the far pasture; something was wrong with the watering tank there, and he had promised to look after it. But the voice was coming nearer.

"Jim! O Jim!"

Suddenly it was within the barn itself, and cramming everything into the box again, Jim shouted, in a tone not too pleasant, "All right! I'm comin'," and bolted down the ladder.

"What was it kept you?" his father asked.

"Nuthin' much," Jim answered, noncommittally.

His father did not pursue the subject. "Hurry," he said. "A swarm of bees is in the box elder just by the tool shed. The limbs are too light for me to climb. You'll make it all right."

Jim followed his father, sullen and resentful. It was not pleasant to be called from his dreams back to this prosaic farm world; and yet the hiving of a swarm of bees did offer some excitement. A fellow might get stung; and Jim was ready for desperate chances. On the ground beneath the tree they placed the new hive. From the shed Jim brought a saw and a light rope; then, scorning a bee veil, he stepped from his father's hand to his father's shoulder, so to the roof of the shed, and swung aloft into the branches. The swarm was clustered thick upon an outjutting limb twenty feet from the ground; he worked his way toward it, knotted the cord about the branch, sawed through it cautiously and then, more cautiously still, lowered it to his father, who was waiting below. When Jim reached the ground, the bees were already taking possession of their new quarters. He and his father carried the hive to the bee yard and set it up there.

"Have you fixed the tank yet?" his father asked.

"Not yet," he answered.

"Better look at it," said his father.

Father always talked like that—just suggesting, you would have said, but the things that he suggested had to be done. Sullenly, resentfully, Jim started off for the far pasture. On his way he picked up a stick, and as he walked he slashed savagely at the weeds. It was always this way. "Come, Jim. Go, Jim. Jim hadn't you better do this? Hadn't you better do that?" Always at his father's beck and call! And what did he get? A candid friend might have suggested a full year's schooling; Jim failed to get that. But Jim would probably have replied that school was only another, and not always a better, form of slavery. The friend might have suggested three regular and abundant meals each day, sufficient clothes, a clean bed, and the companionship of a good and variable man; but it is doubtful if Jim in his present mood would have admitted much value in any of his present surroundings, least of all his father's companionship. What he wanted was freedom, freedom from all orders and restraints, not that he saw clearly just what he would do with his freedom; he could not quite imagine what it would be like, but he wanted it anyhow, and he meant to have it.

Repairing the tank, which served as a watering trough for the cattle in the far pasture, he found a simple matter. The outlet was clogged with dead leaves; the water had overflowed and made of the ground about it a mudhole in which the cattle stood knee-deep. Once he had cleared the opening, the water flowed as it should; a few hot days would dry up the mud.

He turned back toward the house. A sense of vast emptiness told him that it must be near suppertime. After supper would come the milking—the never-ending routine again. He glanced toward the cow barn, and the sight of it brought a disquieting thought. Had he locked his box? Swiftly he mounted the haymow, found the box—no, it was not locked—thrust his hand inside, and touched the barrel of the revolver. Had he not put that in first and laid the knapsack on top? He would have vowed—

"Jim! O Jim!"

He muttered an impatient word. Must it always be like this? Always somebody to call him? He took all the time he wanted to lock and secrete the box carefully. Then he climbed down the ladder, and found his father talking with three strangers who had just arrived in a dust-covered car.

"This is my boy," Mr. Boyd said to them. "Jim, this is Mr. and Mrs. Kurtz. You won't remember them, but they were our near neighbors in Fenton. This is Ned; he and you were born in the same month."

Jim was shy of strangers; they made him conscious of his hands and feet, conscious of his clothes, though Ned's clothes were no better than his own Sunday suit.

He shook hands with them, mumbled replies to their questions, and endured their comments on his growth and size.

"And just to think," Mrs. Kurtz bubbled, "we might have gone right past. I said to Will not ten miles back, 'It's up here somewhere that Colvin Boyd lives.' But we had no idea just where it was, and then came that blowout, and we turned in here to fix it—never even saw the name on the mail box—and there you stood. Why, it seems too good to be true!"

Her husband's eyes had roved from the house to the barns and out over the fields. "A nice place you've got here, Colvin," he observed.

"I can't complain," Mr. Boyd answered, "but you know it isn't quite ours yet."

"Mortgaged?"

"Most farms about here are. Him and I will work it out someday. You'll stay all night with us?" he added.

Husband and wife both protested.

"To supper, then," he insisted. "Jim, maybe you can help Ned fix up that tire. Jennie and Will, come right in now. I'm going to get supper."

"Indeed you're not," retorted Mrs. Kurtz. "*I'm* going to get supper! Just show me where you keep your things. It's been a week now since I have cooked in a real kitchen, but I haven't forgotten."

Out of hearing of the boys, her voice took a more serious tone. "How has it been, Colvin?" she asked. "Will and I've talked of you, I don't know how often. You haven't written much, you know. Well, neither have we, but how have you got on? You and the boy are here all alone?"

"Not quite alone," he answered gravely. "A woman comes in once a week to bake and clean for us. Most of the time we're too busy to think much about things."

"But it isn't—"

"It isn't what it would have been if Margaret had lived. Sometimes it seems to me I miss her more every year."

"Does Jim remember his mother?" Mrs. Kurtz asked.

"I think not. I've told him some things so many times that he thinks he remembers, but I can't believe that he really does! He was less than two, you know, when she died."

"And does he like it here?"

Jim's father paused at the kitchen door

before he answered. "He's a good boy and a good worker, a pretty good worker—as boys go. But there's not the companionship about here that I would like for him. I'm not companionship for him; he needs someone younger, someone more cheerful, more high-spirited. This farm work, the steady grind of it, irks and chafes him. I can see it. At his age it would have been the same with me. But what to do about it—"

He turned to the cupboards. "Here is our larder, such as it is. Eggs, milk, cream, butter—use all of them you like: they are our staples. There are potatoes, and there seems to be plenty of flour. We have our own honey—"

"That is all I want. Warm biscuits and honey, creamed eggs and mashed potatoes. You men can clear right out. Take Will to the barn, Colvin; show him the whole place. I'll send the boys for you when supper is ready."

Jim had never helped mend a tire. That was another thing that disgusted him with the farm—his father would not buy a car. Jim and the agent at Eltonville had argued the point with his father, but always his father had talked of the mortgage. Jim had grown up in the shadow of that mortgage.

He watched Ned lay out the needed tools. Eagerly he followed directions. The tire was removed, the inner tube taken from its casing, the break pronounced too bad to be fixed, and the spare tire was put on. In the course of the work the two boys became pretty well acquainted.

All this, however, did not efface one quite alarming thought, and it came back with renewed force when Ned was called to wash up for supper and Jim's father suggested that he go and let down the bars for the cattle. In that short walk down the lane to the pasture his mind swept the whole problem. He was less and less uncertain. He almost knew that the first thing he had put into his box had been the revolver, and the last thing had been the knapsack. But when he went back the revolver had lain on top. Someone had been there he felt certain, and if so, who but his father?

It was not certain that Jim Boyd had really meant to run away. It was a great source of satisfaction to know that he *could* run away any time he liked. He had his equipment, and week by week he had added the dimes and nickels to his cash resources. Two miles across the fields there was a siding where cattle were sometimes loaded; there he would "jump a freight." This he planned to do sometime in the future perhaps, but now his father had found his box. "If I'm going at all," he said to himself with sudden decision, "I must go tonight and—and I *will*."

It was a wonderful supper. The mere presence of "company" made it remarkable; it was so seldom that they had any guests at the farm. And the food tasted different.

"Father is some cook," Jim said to Ned, "but, believe me, he isn't in it with your mother!"

And Ned answered, "Oh, well, of course—"

It really was not to be expected that anyone, let alone a man, should be in the same class with his mother. The two boys ate themselves full, and then when Mrs. Kurtz was washing dishes and Jim and his father were setting off to milk, nothing would do but that Ned, too, must try his hand at it. He had never milked, to be sure, but then neither had Jim ever helped fix a tire. Ned was just going to try it. They found an old pair of Jim's overalls, and Ned put them on and took his milk pail. Showing him how, and watching the awkward work he made of it—it seemed to Jim that he had never seen anything half so funny! He laughed until the rafters rang; his father laughed, too; Ned's father laughed; Ned himself laughed. Jim could not remember another so jovial a milking.

Several cans of milk must, according to farm schedule, be put through the separator that night, but Mr. Kurtz insisted that Mr. Boyd should have no hand in it. "Leave that to the boys, Colvin," he said. "They'll spell each other. Come in here and sit down."

So the boys took turns at the separator, with the door open into the front room,

whence they caught bits of their elders' talk. In one corner of the front room stood a little cabinet organ that had not been opened since Jim could remember.

"May I play something, Colvin?" asked Mrs. Kurtz. "That is, if you don't mind. You're sure you don't mind?"

As the dusk gathered, she played one old hymn after another.

When it was quite dark and the lamps had been lighted, Mr. Boyd called Jim upstairs. "They're going to stay all night," he said. "Just help me make up the bed."

From the closet they took out bedding long unused, and with it made up the bed in the spare room. At the door the father stopped, lamp in hand. "Just a moment," he said, and Jim's apprehensive heart stood still. He could guess what was coming.

"The Kurtzes are going to Yellowstone National Park." His father's voice was very low and quiet. "They will be gone a month, perhaps, camping on the way. They want me to let you go along."

In after years James Boyd was always glad to remember what came uppermost in his mind's tumult at that moment. "Dad," he said huskily, "do you think—do you think you could spare me?"

"It will be harder, of course, but I guess Chris can give me a little more time. We'll manage somehow."

"There's—there's the mortgage, you know."

"Yes, but it's a very unusual chance and—" his father used a phrase that always settled a matter—"and I think your mother would have wanted it that way."

"Thank you, Dad."

"Only there must be a bargain," his father went on steadily. "We've talked about college. Your mother and I talked about it even before you were born. But while the mortgage hangs on I'm not sure we could make it. If you go this summer, I want you to promise to do your best till it's paid off. Then the next thing will be your schooling."

"And do you know," Captain Boyd said, when he had come to the end of the story, "I went, and I had the most wonderful summer any boy ever had. Lakes, canyons, boiling springs, geysers, rainbow trout, bears within biscuit toss, deer, elk, buffalo! Then I came home and, do you know, the first thing I saw when I climbed up into the haymow was that fool box of mine standing there as plain as a hitching post, as it couldn't help being, with all the hay cleared away! I kicked the lid off and dumped it upside down. The knapsack went to the attic, the knife I pocketed, the money I put in the savings bank—a nest egg for college expenses. The revolver I chucked into Blue River. Then one day I told Dad the whole story.

"It seemed he had never looked into that box of mine, even when his last forkful of hay had uncovered it—I'd invented all that scare for myself. He knew, of course, how I had been feeling. But I played square with Dad after that summer. In three years we had paid off the mortgage. The fourth year I was a freshman in the state university. But think how near I came to missing out! Little fool! But for that flat tire of the Kurtzes I might have been a hobo!"

*A*ll obstetricians know that the first two questions a new mother asks after coming out of the fog of delivery are, "Is it a boy, or a girl?" and "Is it all right?" Of the two, the latter is always the more emotional. That was certainly true of my wife when our two children were born. Fortunately, we didn't have to endure what the parents in this story did.

What a dividing point between the world that was before and the world that was after for them—changing them forever.

SCARS OF TRIUMPH

Barbara Bradford

From my south living room window I saw Mrs. Kaiser cross the road from her house and turn in to our driveway.

"Oh, no," I groaned aloud to myself, "not another one."

But I knew it was. Another someone coming to see the spectacle my new baby and I had become. I picked my baby up and wrapped him in a blanket so only his round little face showed. As I did it I knew that before Mrs. Kaiser left I would have to choose between being downright rude and removing the blanket to show her the little foot that turned down and sideways. A club foot, the doctor called it.

"What a nice surprise," I greeted my neighbor. That was exactly half a lie. The "surprise" was all truth. This was the first time she had crossed the road to call on me. I knew the purpose of this visit was to get a firsthand look at the monstrous mother who would bear a less-than-perfect child and to see for herself just how the child was deformed.

I turned my small son's face toward her. His big dark eyes turned in her general direction.

"Why," she exclaimed in surprise, "he's quite a nice baby, isn't he? You wanted a girl this time, though, I heard. It would have been nice since you already have one boy. But I always think it's better for a boy to be crippled than a girl. You'll probably have trouble with your older boy now. This baby will need so much more care than a normal baby, you won't have time to give the other child the attention he needs. Poor child," she murmured, patting my sturdy two-year-old on the head.

I wished she would go home, but I said as politely as I could, "Won't you sit down?"

She began immediately to pry out the information she had come to get. "I hear your baby nearly died the night he was born," she baited.

"Yes, that's true. We certainly are thankful

he is gaining nicely now!" She seemed to know all there was to know, so there wasn't much for me to say.

"He nearly bled to death, didn't he?" she pried.

I nodded and lifted my baby to my shoulder so I could turn my burning face into his blanket. I waited for the rasping, poking voice to go on, glad that words had no meaning for the little fellow under discussion.

Mrs. Kaiser took her glasses off and polished them with the hem of her dress. She peered at me with her near-sighted eyes. "Had to call the doctor back, didn't you? I heard his car come twice. Your lights were on all night, too. What caused the hemorrhage?"

I couldn't think of a way to dodge that question, and so I replied simply, "The cord had to be retied. It didn't hold the first time."

"Oh, my!" she clucked. "And then on top of that to have him a cripple. How perfectly awful! He gets that from you, doesn't he? I mean the crippled foot. I never realized you were a cripple, too, until someone told me at the store this morning."

"Why, Mrs. Kaiser," I gasped in astonishment, "whoever told you that? It isn't true. There's nothing wrong with my feet or legs."

"There, there, now," soothed Mrs. Kaiser. "Don't get all riled up. I never stopped to think that you might be sensitive about it."

"Look at my legs," I suggested. "There's nothing wrong with them."

"But I saw you limp when you walked over to that chair."

Obviously Mrs. Kaiser would persist until she found out all she wanted to know. Well, then, the quicker it was over the better. "The reason I limp is that I had an internal abscess that put pressure on my pelvic bone. Walking causes me a great deal of pain and will, until the infection is entirely healed. That, however, has nothing to do with my baby's foot."

"No need to get huffy about it," Mrs. Kaiser pouted. "I'm just interested."

I lifted my son out of the blanket and put him over my shoulder again, leaving the tiny feet in the white bootees in full view. I waited silently while my neighbor stared to her heart's content, storing up all the details to dole out over the party line and across her back fence.

Her curiosity satisfied, Mrs. Kaiser left, murmuring conventional phrases—how nice it was to visit with me and do come to see her sometime.

I closed the door and wished I could shut out the world and its Mrs. Kaisers forever. I looked down at the small creature in my arms. "How are we ever going to stand a lifetime of this, Jerry?" I asked him. "All these people poking and jabbing as though we have no feelings."

I wondered where my old friends were. I

had suddenly become a different person to them because my child was not exactly like theirs. At that point the loneliness was as hard to endure as the knowledge that my child was deformed.

Those hard days were made even harder by my husband's poor health. Until Jerry was a week old, Jack had never had a migraine headache. Then the tension and emotional strain of our misfortune brought on a series of headaches so severe that he had to undergo tests for brain tumor and several other conditions before the diagnosis was sure.

Worry about my husband confused my thinking about our child. It was difficult to believe that it was possible for anything to be wrong with a child of mine. Things like that only happen to other people. All my life I had been able to find a way out of unpleasant situations. I kept waiting for a miracle to happen to save me from having to cope with this problem.

Every night I prayed, "Lord, make this the night of miracles. Let me find Jerry's right foot as straight as his left when I get up in the morning."

A couple of days after Mrs. Kaiser's visit my friend Marge dropped in. I was glad to see her. She was a nurse and had assisted with Jerry's birth. She wouldn't be probing the painful areas of my confused feelings. I greeted her with a smile and a happy hello.

Marge's hazel eyes were cool, and icicles hung from her smile.

"What kind of tales have you been telling?" she blurted out.

"Tales? To whom? About what?"

"The things you have been saying about Dr. Barnes could ruin his practice. Who do you think would call him to deliver a baby if they hear this? You know it isn't true, and I'm really surprised you would say such a thing." Marge was about to burst with indignation.

"What was it I said, Marge, and to whom?" I demanded to know.

"Ruth Marshall told me that Agnes Downs told her that you said Jerry almost died the night he was born, because Dr. Barnes doesn't know how to tie a cord properly."

"I never said any such thing! And I haven't seen either Ruth or Agnes since Jerry came!" I explained about Mrs. Kaiser's visit.

"I'm sorry," Marge said contritely. "I should have known you wouldn't say that." She turned her indignation to Mrs. Kaiser's exaggerated gossiping and the people who were so willing to pick it up, enlarge upon it, and pass it on. She was still sputtering when she left.

I had a good cry after Marge was gone. I had tried my best to accept our misfortune bravely, optimistically, cheerfully. But people! It seemed too much to bear. I threw myself across the bed and gave way to a big, moaning, sobbing cry.

The tears helped to wash away some of the despair. I began to see that this thing that had happened to Jerry would call for adjustments, but that it need not spoil all our lives.

"Lord, help me," I prayed. "Everything is all mixed up. I'm lonesome, but I'm afraid of people now. I'm trying to be brave and cheerful, but here I am acting like a coward. Father, please, please help me. I'm too young, too inexperienced to know how to cope with this thing. Give me the kind of faith it takes to live with a thing like this and come out on top."

There was a knock on the door. I slid off the bed, blew my nose, smoothed my hair, and went to answer it. I found the blondest golden blonde I had ever seen, waiting for me.

"Hello, I'm Margaret Kendall," she introduced herself, ignoring my teary face. "We've just moved into the house on the corner. My husband works with your husband, so I thought it would be nice if we could get acquainted too.

"I hear you have two little boys," she said as she sat down. I felt my back begin to stiffen again, wondering what was coming next. "I have two of my own—they're having their naps now. My next-door neighbor was sitting on her porch, and she said she would listen for them while I scooted down here a minute."

"I'm glad you came," I told her, and meant it. I hoped her friendliness would not freeze into embarrassment when she found out I had a child who was "different."

The baby began to fuss, and I brought him to the living room before he could awaken his brother. I laid him on his tummy across my lap and Mrs. Kendall and I went on with our conversation.

Suddenly she exclaimed, "Look at him lift himself up! What a marvelously strong baby!"

The surprise of discovering it was possible for my baby to excel in anything kept me silent. I wondered whether I should tell her about his foot.

"His foot isn't terribly bad, is it?" Mrs. Kendall asked gently. "It can be corrected, can't it?"

"Oh, yes," I replied, clutching at the break in the bleakness of my life that her honest sympathy had created. "It can be corrected. The doctor says we will start with casts when the baby is older, and the foot will straighten out considerably." She had known about my baby's foot before she came, and it hadn't made any difference!

That brief visit made me realize that Jerry was an individual. He was "different," it was true: he had weak points, but he also had strong ones. There would be a place just for him in the world and in God's work. Even if he had two good feet he couldn't fill anyone else's place, or they his.

I remember the hollow feeling I had the day, months later, when the doctor said it was time to begin the casts.

"It doesn't bother the baby nearly as much as it does you," he assured me when he saw the tears rolling down my cheeks. "He will soon forget what it was like without it. You can tell it doesn't hurt him."

Yes, I could tell Jerry was finding the cast more interesting than annoying. I had to hold his hands to keep them from getting wrapped in the cast, too. When it was finished he patted it happily and tried to tell me all about it in his gurgling baby language.

The cast had to be changed every week. Sometimes the doctor would stand with one hand on his bald head, study Jerry's foot, and mutter to himself. Sometimes he said aloud, "I don't understand why it isn't improving faster." Sometimes he would say, "Maybe we ought to stop this"; and then he would change his mind and say, "No, we'll try one more."

Finally he told us frankly that the casts weren't helping. "There's no use going on like this. It's costing you a lot of money, it's restricting the growth of that foot, and it isn't doing any good. We'll wait until he walks and see whether the foot won't straighten out when he puts his weight on it." I wondered when that would be. He was already well past walking age.

We had to review all the procedures with the specialist, Dr. Hawley, at the bone clinic in the city a hundred miles from home.

"Tell me everything about this foot," he commanded. He went on examining Jerry, now two years old and walking a little.

He turned to his secretary. "Miss Kilmartin, write down that I find . . ." A torrent of medical terms followed. Without another word the doctor swept out the door with his secretary trailing after him. We waited, bewildered by the abrupt exit. We wished we had some idea what it was the doctor had found and what we were expected to do.

A sweet-faced, gray-haired lady put her head in the doorway. "Bring your little boy this way, please," she said.

My husband gathered the too-big hospital gown around Jerry and picked him up. I put his clothes over my arm, and we followed the lady until we stopped in front of an elevator.

"X-ray is on the fifth floor, opposite the elevator," the lady explained. "Give the girl at the desk this paper."

When we returned, Dr. Hawley put the X-rays in the lighted frame and studied them carefully.

"Take him to the plaster room," he commanded.

We had ample time to become familiar with the plaster room while we waited. We discussed the clinic and its staff in careful whispers.

"Dr. Hawley scares me to death," I confided to my husband.

"Dr. Hawley is a great man," he replied. "He's the best in his field in this part of the country. He can't take time to chat if he intends to get around to everyone who needs him."

Dr. Hawley and his retinue swirled into the room. A girl started water running into a pan in the sink and while it was filling tied a gown over the doctor's immaculate whites. His red-headed assistant directed us to put Jerry on the table where three interns were gathered to observe. Miss Kilmartin stood near the window, with pencil poised over her notebook.

The doctor rested Jerry's bad foot in his hand and addressed the interns. He talked to them as though we were stone deaf or off on another planet.

"This is what is commonly called a club foot. It is a throw-back to our ancient ancestors. Notice the bone structure . . ." He went on to explain the similarity of Jerry's foot to an ape's.

I wanted to protest, to cry out, "This child is a product of God's creative love, not a chance descendant of some ancient quadruped."

The doctor's voice strode on. "It may be that this foot cannot be permanently corrected with casts. Surgery will then be indicated."

I listened through a fog while he explained in detail how a wedge of bone could be removed from the side of the foot to permit it to turn outward to a normal position. Then another operation would be needed to make the ankle more flexible. I listened with mounting despair as he talked of various bones and rates of growth. From the jumble of medical terms I sifted out the fact that all of what he had been talking about might result in Jerry's right leg being considerably shorter than his left. It would take two more operations to correct that difficulty.

"All right, Miss Swanson," the doctor said, and the plaster team was triggered into action.

The next four years went by in cycles of casts and braces.

"Walk to the door, Sport," Dr. Hawley would tell the barefooted Jerry. "Now back."

He would watch the boy's every movement intently, feel various joints, and then turn his head toward the table where the ever-present Miss Kilmartin sat, with pencil and notebook.

"Continue present program," the doctor's voice might say, and the pencil recorded it. Or "Adjust brace," he would say. On the black days the pencil set down the marks that meant another series of casts.

Our lives were divided into the two weeks, four weeks, six weeks between clinic appointments. Jerry passed his sixth birthday, and after a few more appointments it was September. Jerry went gaily off to school. He couldn't roller skate. He couldn't jump rope. He couldn't run races. But he could learn.

"Take care of him, Lord," I prayed after he was gone. "He's so little and he has already been hurt so much." It was a long time before I could put my mind on my work that morning.

All day I worried about him. Would the other children tease him? Would he try too hard to be like the others and wear himself out with his trying? Would he seek defense in sullenness? Would the effort to keep up with the others discourage him? Would someone brand him with a cruel nickname? Would they call him a cripple?

I had heard that word too much, and how I hated it! "Is it your child who is a cripple?" people would ask. Or perhaps, "How can you let a crippled child go outside to play as if he were normal?"

I firmly believed, and still do, that being a cripple is a state of mind as much as a state of the body, or perhaps more. We were determined that Jerry's mind would be healthy, happy, and unaffected by his misfortune.

The teacher called that evening to report on Jerry's first day in school.

"I knew you would be anxious," she told me. "Jerry got along fine. He acts so natural the other children don't notice he is any different."

The next morning it was easier to smile when I waved to him from the front porch as he turned the corner and went out of sight.

On the next clinic day Miss Kilmartin's pencil made some little marks that put a temporary end to Jerry's school days. "Surgery as soon as possible," the pencil echoed and then was still as the doctor explained what we had known since the day he lectured the interns as if we weren't there. He omitted the bit about the apes, but told us the nature of the operation and expressed his regret that he had not had Jerry's case early enough to correct his deformity with casts. It was obvious that he would rather not subject a child to surgery, that it was a last resort. I knew, then, that he had a heart under his blustery exterior, that he was capable of compassion, and that Jerry would be in gentle hands.

Even so, it was hard to sleep nights while we waited to hear from the hospital. Jerry seemed unconcerned. Partly, we thought, because of the ignorance of childhood, partly because he had already learned it was useless to rebel against the inevitable. I was still battering myself to bits trying to change the unchangeableness of the experience that threatened my son.

I had a moment of panic when I took the

pen from Miss Kilmartin's hand to sign the permit for surgery. I wished my husband had been able to come along. I needed reassurance that we were doing the right thing.

"You couldn't let them operate!" Jerry's grandmother had protested.

"Of course we will," we said. "It has to be done to give Jerry anything at all like a normal life. There is no choice."

As I hesitated over the paper on Miss Kilmartin's desk I realized there was a choice. I could refuse to leave my child. I could take him back home where he could swing in the sun or play in his sand box under the apple tree and sleep in his own bed and be done with all this pain, unhappiness, and worry forever.

Miss Kilmartin cleared her throat, and I glanced up to see her looking at me peculiarly. I gripped the pen more tightly and put my shaky signature on the paper.

"It has to be," I kept telling myself as Jerry and I, holding tightly to each other's hands, followed Miss Kilmartin through the tunnel to the main hospital building. "There is no other way to give Jerry a normal life. This will soon be over—it will, it will, it will—and then there will be a long happy lifetime ahead."

We had played hospital at home, and Jerry was watching with fascinated delight to discover for himself all the things I had told him about. I struggled to rid my throat of the lump and the invisible restricting band and croaked,

"It's nice here, isn't it?"

Jerry turned on his shy, happy smile, and I knew everything was fine with him.

I managed a smile, a little stiff on the edges, with my good-bye. Outside the door, I looked back. Jerry was already playing with the boy in the next bed.

Early the next morning I went to the hospital. The children were sitting up in bed, hanging over the foot, jumping, or actively doing something. All but Jerry. He was still asleep. A card was fastened to his gown with a huge safety pin. On it was his name and the kind and amount of medication he had been given.

I stood beside the white hospital crib and wondered whether I had done the right thing the day before, when I had resisted the impulse to take him home. Was it fair to put him through this ordeal? What if—what if something went wrong and he never came back to me?

"You'll have to have more faith than that," the still small voice within me said. "Let your faith grow large enough to encompass this large trial."

The rubber-wheeled stretcher moved across the room. The orderly roused Jerry enough to make him understand I was there. I walked beside the stretcher holding his hand until the orderly told me I would have to wait on a comfortable divan, and let Jerry go on without me.

"It's all right, Mother," Jerry said with exaggerated slowness from the faraway place where he was floating. "My angel will take care of me."

I spent the long, waiting hours of the morning trying to stretch my faith to match my needs. Good thing I did, too.

The carts with their tinkling loads of dinner trays were moving past me when Jerry came back. I stood beside his bed and fought against being sick. The mixed-up odor of ether, antiseptic, and wet plaster was bad enough, but the change in Jerry was worse— the paleness, the droopy mouth, the limpness of his body. I would have been sure he was dead if I hadn't heard the sound of his rhythmic, deep breathing.

"I'm proud of you, Jerry," Dr. Hawley's assistant told him that night; "you were a brave boy."

She turned to me. "He was completely unafraid. How did you accomplish it?"

I shrugged vaguely. Perhaps the faith I was seeking so desperately had been there all the time for Jerry to absorb and use in his own need.

All winter Jerry wore a cast. There was no sliding with the other children, no "fox and geese," no snowmen—and no complaints. All there was to show he cared was the deep sigh that was the echo of the outdoor children's happy shouts—and a little nose pressed against the window. Perhaps being out of bed after six full weeks of lying completely still, flat on his back, was enough to satisfy him.

A brace came in the spring, and also the census taker. The questions seemed endless. "Dog? Cat?" She started to close the big book and then opened it again. "I almost forgot, I'm supposed to ask if any member of the family is handicapped."

I told her about Jerry.

"You should have that taken care of," the lady said, visibly swelling with authority. "You would be surprised how much can be done to correct a condition like that. I'll have to turn this name in and the authorities will be getting in touch with you. Let's see, what was the child's name?"

Jerry came down the sidewalk with the little hippity-hop that substituted for a run. He bounded up the steps and stood grinning at my elbow.

"This is Jerry," I said. I watched her look him over from head to—oh-oh, a brace.

"Oh, I see he has medical attention. That's good." She made a check mark in her book and slithered out of sight.

Three years later Miss Kilmartin's pencil jotted notes that meant another operation. It would be performed on a different part of the foot, but everything else would be the same, we thought.

We had a huge surprise in store for us. A

revolution had taken place in the medical profession. The doctors no longer believed it necessary for a surgical patient to stay totally inactive. As soon as the pain had let up and the danger of swelling inside the cast was past, Jerry was allowed to sit up. He could come into the living room and be one of the family if someone carried him. (Ever try to carry a nine-year-old boy complete with twenty pounds of cast?)

Another three years passed before Dr. Hawley said, "Well, sport, I had hoped we could avoid this, but we can't. There is too much difference in the lengths of your legs. We'll have to put a pin in your left leg to slow the growth until the right leg is able to catch up."

I marveled at a science that could perform such miracles and at the goodness of God, that He would allow an avowed atheist to use so great a gift. But I grieved over the fact that my son must suffer still more. There was no getting used to that. Each time the surgeon's knife operated, it brought a fresh sting to my heart.

Jerry had grown so tall he was put in the larger bed in the men's ward. I was determined to maintain absolute control of my emotions before all those adult eyes. For six solid hours I did. Then when the man in the bed next to Jerry's offered me something to eat, commenting, "You look beat," I burst

into a flood of tears. The next operation came sooner than anticipated. One of the pins was working itself out. Dr. Hawley studied the X-rays, consulted his partner, Dr. Foran, and announced, "We'll operate next week."

But Dr. Hawley didn't operate the next week. He had a heart attack and was in critical condition on the second floor of the hospital. I prayed for his recovery. He got well and lived several more years, but we never saw him again.

Dr. Foran performed Jerry's operation. It was Dr. Hawley's assistant who removed the cast for the last time. She remembered the first day we had come to the clinic twelve years before, and she reminisced as the power saw chewed the cast off Jerry's leg.

"Remember the old hand cutters we used to use to remove a cast? Now just a few zips with this thing and it's done. You know, you have been around here almost as long as I have. I'm going to miss you."

It took a while to get used to marking time by the calendar instead of by clinic appointments. With the passing of the years, many people have forgotten anything was ever wrong with Jerry. There are only a few things to remind them—the right shoe four sizes smaller than the left, refusals of ice-skating invitations, and a loping kind of run in a ball game.

Jerry has a toboggan but no skis. He swims

while others water-ski. But he can whirl around the college gym floor on his specially adapted roller skates. He can build a garage or write a poem. He can pour cement and sing in the choir. He can dream of the day when he will be trained to minister to the sick with the hands that learned compassion the hard way.

There are perhaps more signs of Jerry's misfortune in my heart than on his body. The wounds Mrs. Kaiser, and people like her, inflicted have healed over and left sympathy and understanding in place of resentment and bitterness. My wall of self-defense has crumbled into a cloud of compassion that envelops all afflicted ones. In the quiet hospital waiting rooms, I found patience I didn't know existed.

But best of all, in the dark valley I found faith and trust. With all my heart I say, "Thank You, Lord, for loving us enough to send us a trial severe enough to make us seek refuge in You." The happiest days I have known are not one half so precious to me as the darkest. It was in the darkness that I saw God most clearly.

By 1966, we will have repaid the loans that financed those four operations. Then there won't be much left to remind us of the past—except the scars on Jerry's foot and on my heart. We wouldn't exchange those scars for anything in this world. They are the marks of our triumph.

*F*ailure—nothing but failure. Might as well give up! But that was before a man he'd never heard of before took time to show him the far side of failure.

In college, I'm sorry to say, I was initially happy if I made Cs. Later on, I received a smattering of Bs. That wasn't so hard, *I said to myself.* But As were away off into the stratosphere—not for the likes of me. But on one never-to-be-forgotten day, I got an A– in a history class. *I just couldn't believe it!* Me—capable of an A–? *So, if I worked just a bit harder, perhaps I could get an A without the minus.* Amazingly, from that day forth, through a bachelor's degree, two master's degrees, and the doctorate—almost never did I again earn a grade lower than A.

This story is excerpted from Arthur Gordon's best-selling book, A Touch of Wonder.

ON THE FAR SIDE OF FAILURE

Arthur Gordon

At the age when you're convinced you can twist the world into a pretzel, I left my native Georgia and got a job, a very small job, on a New York magazine. I intended to be a writer. I figured that I would learn exactly what sort of writing was in demand; then I would quit my job, start producing reams of this precious commodity, and shortly retire to the Riviera to hobnob with Noel Coward and Somerset Maugham.

It didn't quite work out this way. The things I wrote at night or on weekends came bouncing back with dismal regularity. At the end of a year the record showed nothing but consistent failure.

Well, if I wasn't cut out to be a writer, I told myself, *I could at least take over the magazine business.* To hasten this process, every noon I would go to the automat, buy a bun, take it out to a bench in Central Park, and dream great dreams.

One day, munching on my bun, I began to wonder why my employer, who owned a whole flock of magazines, didn't translate some of his better magazine articles into Spanish, combine them into a single top-quality magazine, and assign a star salesman—me—to sell it all over Latin America. It was such a splendid vision that I arose with a shout, scattering my bun crumbs to the startled pigeons, and hurried back to my cubbyhole at the office.

Of course, there might be problems in the form of tariffs, currency regulations, and so on. Before approaching the boss with my brilliant idea, I decided to find out about these details. I asked my cellmate at the office if he knew of an authority on Latin America.

"Latin America?" he said. "I guess T. J. Watson over at IBM knows as much about Latin America as anyone. They do tremendous business down there."

"IBM?" I echoed. "What's that?" I thought it might be a federal agency like the WPA, which was flourishing at the time.

He gave me a look of weary scorn.

"International Business Machines. Why don't you go back to Georgia?"

Well, I had never heard of International Business Machines, or this T. J. Watson either. But certainly he had to eat, and if I was careful, I figured, I could afford two buns in the park—or maybe even the cafeteria at the zoo.

So I called up IBM and asked for Mr. Watson. When a secretarial voice answered, I announced cheerily that I would like to buy Mr. Watson a lunch and pick his brains about Latin America. I'd been told he was an authority, I explained. Friday would suit me best. (It was payday.) We would eat in the park, I said, not specifying the menu. I could pick Mr. Watson up at his office, or we could meet at the zoo.

"The zoo?" echoed the voice, with rising inflection.

"The cafeteria at the Central Park Zoo," I said a bit impatiently. "Will you go and ask him, please?"

The voice went away, but soon came back. Mr. Watson would be glad to see me, it said. But he had suggested that I come and have lunch with him. In the light of my finances, this struck me as a first-rate suggestion.

When I walked into the IBM skyscraper on Fifty-Seventh Street and asked the elevator man if he happened to know on which floor someone named T. J. Watson worked, he gave me a queer look and a number. On the designated floor, the receptionist summoned a secretary who took me to a waiting room. There another secretary came and escorted me to another waiting room. Each time the paneling grew darker and richer, the pile of the carpet deeper, and the reverential silence more profound. So did my conviction that somebody was making a terrible mistake—probably me.

The final secretary was a man. "The president will see you now," he said pleasantly.

"President?" I said hoarsely. But already a massive door had swung open, revealing an office roughly the size of Grand Central Station. At the far end, behind an enormous, polished desk, was a tall, silver-haired gentleman: Thomas J. Watson, Senior, one of the mightiest tycoons in America. On his desk was a small, neatly lettered sign. "THINK," it said. I *was* thinking—thinking I should have stayed in Georgia.

He rose with as much courtesy as if I had been a visiting ambassador. "Well, young man," he said, "it's nice of you to drop in. Sit down and tell me what I can do for you."

I moved forward like a man in a trance and sat down. But I was speechless.

He waved his hand. "Don't let these surroundings bother you. When I was about your age, I was working in a store in an upstate town named Painted Post, trying to sell pianos and organs. Backgrounds change, but people don't—much. Now tell me: What's all this about Latin America?"

My voice came back from wherever it had gone, and I told him about my plan. He listened attentively. I said that I wanted to know what difficulties to expect.

He nodded. "It's not a bad idea at all. I'll arrange for you to see the right people after lunch." He touched a button, and a little man appeared with a notebook. On the notebook cover, I noticed, was a word stamped in gold: "THINK."

Mr. Watson named the people I was to see. "And while you're at it," he added casually, "see that this young man gets a copy of every magazine published in Latin America." (They came, too. In droves.)

"Now," said Mr. Watson, "how about some lunch? I really was tempted to meet you at the zoo. Nobody ever asked me to the zoo for lunch before. But we have our own dining rooms here, and the habit of time-saving is hard to break."

Mr. Watson and I had a fine lunch. He told me about IBM, its vast worldwide organization, the benefits for employees, the little copybook maxims that he liked to hang on office and factory walls. People didn't notice them consciously after a while, he admitted, but unconsciously they were affected by them. "THINK" was one of his favorites. "AIM HIGH" was another. "You were aiming pretty high," he said quizzically, "when you said you wanted to pick my brains. But I like that. That's why I said yes."

I admitted, with a gulp, that when I walked into the building I hadn't the faintest idea who he was. He laughed. "It's a blow to my ego, but probably a healthy one." He looked at me speculatively. "How much salary are you making now?"

I told him. It didn't take long.

He smiled. "If you'd like to join our IBM family, I think we could do a little better for you than that."

"Thank you, sir," I said, "but machines don't like me. What I want to be eventually is . . ." I stopped. I had about decided that I would never be a writer. But I had a feeling that this man could see right through me anyway, so I told him about the year of writing failures, the endless rejection slips.

He leaned back in his chair. "It's not exactly my line," he said, "but would you like me to give you a formula for writing success?" He hesitated. "It's quite simple, really. Double your rate of failure."

I stared at him. This was no copybook maxim.

"You're making a common mistake," he said. "You're thinking of failure as the enemy of success. But it isn't at all. Failure is a teacher—a harsh one, perhaps, but the best.

You say you have a desk full of rejected manuscripts? That's great! Every one of those manuscripts was rejected for a reason. Have you pulled them to pieces looking for that reason? That's what I have to do when an idea backfires or a sales program fails. You've got to put failure to work for you."

He folded his napkin and put it beside his plate. "You can be discouraged by failure—or you can learn from it. So go ahead and make mistakes. Make all you can. Because, remember, that's where you'll find success. On the far side of failure."

I did remember. My desk was still full of unsalable manuscripts. And when I presented my grand design for a Latin American magazine to the boss, he said acidly, "Do you think we have money to put into a crazy scheme like this? Stop bothering me." (Actually, it wasn't such a bad idea. A year or two later *Reader's Digest* started its Spanish and Portuguese editions, which today are the most widely circulated magazines in Latin America.)

But that's not the point. The point is that somewhere inside me a basic attitude had shifted. A project turned down, a lot of rejected manuscripts—why, these were nothing to be ashamed of. They were rungs in a ladder—that was all. A wise and tolerant man had given me an idea. A simple idea, but a powerful one: If you can learn to learn from failure, you'll go pretty much where you want to go.

*H*ave you ever said to yourself, I must speak to ___, and tell her how much I appreciate all she's done! *or* What an impact that boy is having on this community! I must tell him how much we love him for it.

But we get busy, and the words are never said. Perhaps this story will cause us to speak, next time, before it is too late.

The Stranger Within Thy Gates

Author Unknown

"Did you notice that young man who occupied the corner in the back pew during the morning service?" inquired Mrs. Murray of her husband, as they lingered at the tea table one bright Sunday evening.

"Yes; I was just going to speak of him. He occupied the same place last Sunday morning, and attracted my attention particularly because he was such a good listener," the pastor replied, quietly. "I meant to speak to him at the close of the service, but he was gone before I could reach him."

"It is a pity, for he seemed so alone," answered Mrs. Murray. "Do you know his name?"

"I am sorry I do not. I made inquiry about him last Sunday evening, but no one seemed to know where he was from, or what he was doing in this town. If he comes again, I must not miss him."

But he did, and in precisely the same way that he had done on two former occasions.

The pastor intended to grasp his hand and give him a cheering word, but while he was busy here and there, the young stranger was gone, and that without exchanging words with a living soul.

The pastor again lamented the neglect as he walked home by the side of his wife, and in his disappointment expressed the hope that some other one had taken the young man by the hand and bidden him welcome. But no one had.

"I shall try to see him during the week, and invite him to come to my class next Sunday," he said, trying to make amends with his conscience for the opportunity he had missed. "Yes, I shall not let another week pass by without making his acquaintance," he added; but how little he knew of the opportunities which the coming week should deny!

That very night, just as the clock struck twelve, a horseman, riding furiously, halted at the parsonage gate, and in a frightened voice, begged the minister to come without delay to the bedside of this same young man, George Fulton, who was dying.

In a very few moments Mr. Murray was speeding toward the lumber camp, where he learned the young man was employed, but never before did the familiar road seem so long, and never before, even in the darkness, did his trusty mare make so many false steps. When at last the house where George was lying was reached, it was only to learn that it was too late—that the opportunity of pointing a brother to Christ was gone forever.

The people at the camp knew very little about the young stranger, except that he was quiet and well-behaved, and always took the heavier end of the timbers when there was lifting to be done; indeed, he prided himself on his fine physique and great strength, and it was to this very natural pride that the physician laid the cause of his sudden death.

On the Friday preceding, the men in the camp had been testing their strength by lifting heavy weights, and he had complained a little of overstrain at the time, but until he awoke in the night with the hemorrhage that speedily terminated fatally, no serious consequences were apprehended by himself or others. His wish to have the minister called had been gratified, but half an hour before the messenger returned, poor George Fulton had died.

From a little diary that the father of the dead boy put into his hand on the day of the funeral, Mr. Murray learned that it was his loneliness that had driven him to the house of God on the first day, and that something in the sermon on that morning had set him to thinking seriously of the careless life he had been leading. Again and again he went without receiving either the comfort or the aid he sought, and then before the welcome words that had been lingering on the pastor's lips—the words he fully meant to speak—had been uttered, he was gone, his lifework was ended, and the opportunity of helping a struggling brother heavenward had passed forever.

All this the young pastor felt, and that day, as he stood by the coffin of the stranger who had passed away without so much as a smile of recognition, he vowed to be more faithful in the future. A full decade has passed since that grave on the hillside was dug, and the vow then made has been faithfully kept. No stranger is allowed to visit Mr. Murray's church, even for a single service, without receiving a warm handclasp and a kind word to cheer him on his way.

The lesson learned by the coffin of the young lumberman was never forgotten, and though it came too late to be of aid to him, it has helped others—wayfarers tarrying for perhaps but a day—to lay their burdens down at Jesus' feet, and in their stead to bear a joyful song away.

Life is too short to miss a single opportunity

of giving a cup of cold water in the Master's name; hence, in imitation of Him who came not to be ministered unto, but to minister, let us bid Godspeed to the stranger within our gates, not knowing but that we may thereby help a struggling brother into the light.

"Inasmuch as ye have done it unto one of the least of these my brethren, ye have done it unto me" (Matthew 25:40, KJV).

I have no idea as to the origins or authorship of this story—but every word in it rings true. I know because when I travel, I watch people, and, since they are often in close proximity to me, overhear what some of them say. I've even spoken to a number of them who appear to be searching for what they don't have. Just listening to some of these stories can be life changing; just as is true with the narrator of this one: she could never again be the person she was when she first walked into this train station.

OUT OF FOCUS

Author Unknown

The waiting room of the union station was crowded as always. Every departing train seemed to thin the restless group, but every incoming train brought in as many more.

A young woman, obviously just arriving, took her place in line at the information desk. And when her turn came, she spoke quietly but anxiously.

"When can I get a train for the East?"

"Eleven forty, Miss," she was told.

And Helen Dawson made way for the next in line. A long evening, especially for one alone in a strange city. She would have time for a little entertainment, to be sure, but Helen was a trifle particular about her entertainment. Besides, she was tired and she felt safer here in the waiting room, lost in the crowd.

Oh yes, she was hungry, too. A few minutes to freshen up, and she would soon take care of that.

Helen sat down at the table near the corner. She had always hated being conspicuous. She glanced quickly about her. Now for a good meal.

But it was not long before she wondered if perhaps she had been too successful in her desire to be unnoticed. Although she really did not mean to eavesdrop, it was apparent that the two people at the next table did not know she was there.

"But Dad, it's a real chance," the younger man was saying.

"A chance for what, my boy? Money?"

"Of course. And right now, you and Mother need it. Both of you have been sacrificing all your lives, and where is it getting you? The idea of wanting to be a nobody in a small town, a country doctor, when you can have a position like this here in the city. Why, Dad, it's foolish. Don't go back. Please don't. Send Mother a telegram, and she'll look after everything. George will help her."

"My boy, I'm afraid—"

"Afraid of what?"

"I'm afraid I've failed to teach you the one thing I wanted you to learn above everything else: a sense of values. Listen Son—" something in the older man's tone seemed to soften the boy.

"Yes, Dad."

"Perhaps I'm a nobody, as you say; perhaps I'm making a wrong decision. But I don't think so. It pleases me to be offered such a place. But I would not be happy were I to accept it. To be sure, it means money, security, social position, prestige—perhaps eventually fame. But I don't desire any of these, son.

"My patients would be rich, and there would be no writing off of bad accounts. My days would be crowded—visits, operations, interviews, talking with those who enjoy being invalids, operating on rich women who want another operation to boast about, interviewing people who don't need a doctor. What more of those rich city patients need is something to do besides twiddle their thumbs. I suppose some of my women patients would fall in love with me. Sounds silly, I know, Son, but a doctor complex is a common disease among certain classes. No, there's no amount of money large enough to make me see it differently. I am not needed here. Back home, many times I am.

"And Son, not until you are a doctor yourself will you understand that a true doctor's greatest joy comes in being needed. There are plenty of physicians in the city, good ones, for those who are sick; but at home, you know the story. The glamour of a bigger job keeps luring doctors away from the small towns. And the people there are poor; often they're sick. And sometimes they can't pay, though they are honest and appreciative, and want to pay. But when somebody gets pneumonia or appendicitis, or a broken leg, or when a baby decides to be born, they've got to have a doctor, got to have one there in town. There is no time to drive forty miles."

"But Dad, you must think of yourself. You've your own life to live."

"Son, when that telephone rings in the middle of the night and somebody cries, 'Hurry, Doc, there's been an accident,' I can't stop to ask who it is, or how his bank account stands. I think, *What if it's my own boy?* And I know that if it were you, and I could save your life, it would be worth more than any amount of wealth or fame. And then I say to myself, *Doc, if it isn't your boy, it's somebody else's boy; his life is just as important to some father, somewhere.*"

"I think I see, Dad. I guess I haven't had a sense of values. I always thought the greatest men were the ones you hear the most about. But I was wrong, Dad," and the boy's voice faltered, "and I'm proud to be the son of a truly great man."

The two men rose from the table. Helen hoped they would not notice her. Her eyes were moist. That was something to think about, that—what had he called it? Sense of values.

Once again in the waiting room, the young woman settled down with a magazine. Two more hours. Somehow, though, she did not read much. She kept thinking about what she had heard. And then there were voices. Helen looked up and saw that she was hidden from the newcomer by a post. *I'm not going to move now,* she told herself. *Perhaps I'll learn something from this conversation, too.* But for a moment she doubted it. What were they saying?

"Yes, I really had a grand time. Didn't you?"

"On the whole, yes. It's the first time I've been back to the college since I graduated."

"Me too. You know, Jane, of course it's different with you. You're a nurse, and you're doing something with your life, giving something to the world. But somehow I've come to the conclusion that I made a great mistake."

"Whenever did you make a mistake? I've always thought you had remarkably good judgment."

"When I married Jim."

"Why, whatever has got into you? You love him, don't you? You have your home and two lovely children. What more could you want?"

"That's all true, Jane, but I feel that I've lost something; I feel I'm getting stale. I never need any particular intellectual ability for my job. Any ordinary woman could do what I do."

"But your children!"

"Any woman can bring children into the world. That isn't anything unusual. I want to be somebody, to do something big in the world. And I might have if I hadn't married Jim."

"But Edna my dear. Oh I see your train is ready. Hope you have a good trip."

"I'll send you my new address soon, Jane."

"New address? Are you moving?"

"Well, I'll tell you. I keep thinking about that lecture the other day and about so many things at the college. Look at Cecilia Wilson. She's made a name for herself. I must be going. But I've made up my mind. I'm going to leave Jim and go on with my study—as I always planned before I met him."

"Edna please—I do hope you'll think it over. Don't you think it's being a little selfish to put developing your own mind and making a name for yourself above being a wife to a good husband and a mother to two darling girls who need you?"

As the two women disappeared in the crowd, Helen was thoughtful. And somehow she felt very sorry for two little girls who were going to have to grow up and fight their way all alone in the world, just because their mother wanted to be somebody—strange cruel world. How she hoped that someone would be able to show that woman that she was wrong, that nothing in the world could be half so important as two little girls whose future, whose eternity, perhaps hung at this moment in her hands.

Helen closed the magazine. It did not seem to fit in with the atmosphere of her thoughts. She had always been a good girl but never deeply religious. As she reflected now, suddenly she wished she had been. These conversations had set her thinking about things that looked large and were small—and things that looked small, but were large. The important things in life seemed to be weighing themselves in her mind against unimportant things. Essentials, nonessentials. How was one to know? And yet everyone she knew must choose every day. A day has only so many hours. What a pity if those hours are ever so busy and yet do not include the truly important things. One must learn to discriminate to see things as they really are, not as they look.

Helen thought about the Bible story she had heard when she was a child, of twelve men who were sent out as spies. Ten of them could see only the walls and the giants, and only two of them saw the land in its true light, a land that could be conquered. They knew that the walls and the giants meant nothing.

Only one thing was important—that God was on their side.

Helen glanced at the clock. Only one more hour. Another train had arrived. People were finding seats here and there. A tall man with a kindly face was coming toward her. Seats were well filled. She moved her coat so that he might sit down.

"Do you mind if I take this seat?" he said politely.

"Of course not," Helen replied, still thoughtful.

"It's tiresome waiting, isn't it?" the man remarked presently. He appeared about seventy years of age.

"Yes, although sometimes it's interesting just watching the people that come and go."

"I quite agree with you there. It has always been my belief that we can learn a great deal from those about us, if we observe closely."

"Yes, if we can see things clearly—not out of focus."

"May I ask what you mean?"

Helen was not in the habit of carrying on conversations of any length with strangers. But something in the man's face seemed to portray deep thinking. He was not just an average person. Perhaps he was a scientist, or a professor. And perhaps she could learn from him. So she went on.

"Well, I hardly know how to explain it myself. Frankly, I overheard two conversations tonight that have set me thinking. Perhaps you'll understand better if I tell you briefly about them."

When she had finished, he said thoughtfully, "Yes, I understand. Too many of us are altogether too busy from daylight till dark doing things that aren't important at all. We can't see to select properly, shall I say? And I suppose we should go on that way indefinitely were it not that something at last wakes us up to the folly of it all. That, to be honest, is why I'm leaving work for a few weeks."

"Yes?"

"You see, I am the pastor of a large city church. I am considered successful—a good speaker, a good promoter. My churches always run smoothly, and make their quotas, and in general are a credit to me. Or at least I thought so up until last week. Then something happened.

"I was called to the bedside of a dying woman. When I arrived it was plain she had at most a few days to live. 'Pastor,' she said, 'I have listened to every word you spoke. You preached some wonderful sermons, pastor, and you explained a lot of things that were hard to understand before. And I've tried to follow all you said, and I've given all the money I could. But I'm going to die. And I'm not a Christian.'

"She sank into unconsciousness before I could speak. I was glad, because I was so ashamed. Suddenly it was all clear to me. I had spent my time promoting this project and that. From the pulpit I gave long explanations of texts. And I talked about the modern trend—from automobiles to hats. But I never talked once on anything on which they could die. I had preached about everything but Christ and the cross, and this one theme I should have made supreme."

"How about the dying woman?"

"Well, I spent a good deal of time with her the next few days, until she passed away. I tried to help her to take hold of Jesus Christ, to see that He was the one thing needful. I believe she accepted Him. But all the time I realized that I had covered Him with explanations and theories and arguments and what not, until I couldn't reach Him myself. So I did the only thing I knew to do. I asked for a few weeks leave of absence, and I'm going to get away where I can think and get a new hold. I've got to preach Christ from now on, and I can't preach about someone I've never known."

"I know you'll succeed," Helen said sincerely. "The greatest lesson we have to learn, I suppose, is a sense of values."

"You are very right—a sense of what is important and what is not. Just working isn't enough. We must be working the right things. You remember the story of the Boy Jesus, how He tarried behind in Jerusalem and was not missed till His parents had gone a day's journey toward home. They supposed He was in good company. And I had supposed He was in good company, too—in the church. How many of us have lost Jesus while we were busy here and there."

"I keep thinking of that doctor and his son. I suppose a good many people will think the man is foolish to turn down the proposition offered him," Helen said.

"Probably so, probably so. He's giving up everything from the world's viewpoint. But then, think of Jesus Himself—all Heaven at His feet, all the worlds about Him that He had created, His subjects. And yet He left it all to come down to this speck of a world to save fallen man. He didn't have to. Certainly He had great and important work in the courts above from the human standpoint. He might be called unwise. True, He accomplished great good by His death—there were a good many people saved. Yet I firmly believe He would have left everything and died just as He did, had there been only one soul to save."

Helen was silent a moment. "Then—certainly a lesson on the value of a human soul. I wish that woman who was going to leave her home and those two little girls—could see that."

"Let us both pray that she may yet understand it. But I see it is time for my train. So I shall say goodbye. I have enjoyed our conversation this evening."

"And I feel that I have learned from it," came the response. "Good-bye."

Helen Dawson boarded her train at 11:40 with these words uppermost in her thoughts: "What shall it profit a man if he shall gain the whole world, and lose his own soul?" (Mark 8:36, KJV).

SECTION TWO

"How frail is humanity!
How short is life, how full of trouble!
We blossom like a flower and then wither.
Like a passing shadow, we quickly disappear."
—Job 14:1, 2, NLT

The east wind of circumstance may drive you often from your course. The tide may go out sometimes and leave you stranded. You may mistake lesser beacons for the great Bishop Light that marks the main channel, but in every dark discouragement that challenges progress, cast out the anchors of faith and wait for the day. And when it comes, as it always must, you will find the faces of truth and God's path through the sea of trouble.

—Harry Moyle Tippett

I had just been fired for the first time in my life, and it felt as though the very foundations of my world were collapsing under me. I had been on such a roll: two master's and doctoral degrees, full professorships in two colleges, chairing English departments in two colleges, directing an adult degree program, presiding over a public school district, leading out in the county United Way, becoming the foremost authority on the life of the frontier writer Zane Grey, and on and on. And now—to be fired after all this!

As I sat there in our dream home, our Shangri-la, a thousand feet above Boulder, Colorado, I thought back, wondering where and how the train of my life had left the track. Had it been because I'd been blinded by too many successes in a row? Had it been because I lusted for higher pay and success in yet another career track? Had I moved ahead of God's plan for my life? In short, had it all degenerated into hubris?

I thought back through the last several years of career restlessness that had led to this day—was it ill-advised for me to have left the rather safe world of academia for a world I knew nothing about: hospital administration? I'd been reveling in being on top of the world, buying a dream chalet in the Rockies, doubling my salary, and living what I considered "the good life." And then, suddenly, it was all over: I'd burned my academic bridges, and, by my failure in this hospital, closed the doors to similar positions in that career as well. Had God let me down? Or had *I* let God down?

Across the room sat the love of my life, Connie, who had entrusted her life to me. Sleepless night had followed sleepless night, with tears and anguish on both sides of the bed. We'd come to a double dead end: no road ahead and no road back.

Suddenly, a knock on our door.

We opened it—and there stood Milton Murray, the grand old man of American fundraising, respected and revered everywhere. Of course, we welcomed him in. For after all, he was the one whose enthusiastic recommendation had led to the fund-raising position in the first place. He'd come prepared. Evidently, I was but another in a long line of fund-raising administrators who'd lost their jobs and felt up the proverbial creek without a paddle. Such a long line, in fact, that he had printed copies of two chapters from a book titled *Who Waits in Faith*: "Too Soon to Quit" and "To Bleed Awhile . . . and Fight Again." These he now handed to me, saying, "Read these, *study* them. . . . I strongly believe they'll give you the courage to move beyond your current despondency and, with God's help, make a brand new start." Then we knelt down by our massive three-story-high moss-rock fireplace, and he prayed that we would entrust our future to the good Lord, and follow His leading. Then he left us, promising to stay in touch.

Afterward, I practically memorized those two chapters. Some of the gems I stalled-out on include these:

If there is anything the youth of today need to learn well, it is the truth that the quitter never wins and the winner never quits.[1]

Following faithfully on never leads anyone into permanent darkness. But for the quitter, all he is likely to get is a stronger habit of quitting and a lower place to begin again. The man who will not give up, even if he fail of his objective, is led through to another objective; the man who hangs on as if he were paid to hang on can always start again at par or better—he has strengthened himself.[2]

Just keeping on, through the most hopeless aspect of keeping on, may be the important act of one's career. The last dejected effort often becomes the winning stroke. After years of observation one is ready to say that most of the people one has seen quit have quit too soon. . . . Quitting makes a dead end of any road—often just as it was ready to open.[3]

One good rule to keep in mind is that there are no crises with God, for no human problem can baffle His wisdom.[4]

Already, reading through this inspirational first chapter, I felt I'd undergone a 180-degree attitudinal change. Then I turned my attention to the book's last chapter. In it, Tippet refers to a rectorial address famed author James M. Barrie gave at Scotland's St. Andrew's University. In it, he referenced some lines from an old British ballad:

Fight on, my men, said Sir Andrew
  Barton.
I am somewhat hurt but am not
  slaine,
I'll lie me down and bleed awhile,
And then I'll rise and fight againe.

To bleed awhile . . . and fight again—here is the formula for all the sublime victories of the soul. In every age it is compounded of those free things of the spirit that never perish. It is the herald of tomorrow's triumph, no matter how desolating today's defeat. It is a challenge to fear and to every other bogey of the mind that makes man lay down his arms even before he has begun to fight.

The battles of life are lost or won in our minds, for it is the decisions we muster that make or mar achievement, that call for resolute advance or cowering retreat, that lead to spiritual eminence or the valley of despair.[5]

The easy chair may beckon to quiet retirement and a yielding of one's place to more aggressive forces, but no one ever left footprints on the sands of time while wearing carpet slippers, and that should be a reminder that as long as time is a talent it is too soon to quit.[6]

By this time, I was increasingly fascinated by the man who wrote these two chapters. I discovered that he was a renowned professor of English at Michigan's Andrews University, and that he had penned a number of books that had continued to inspire down through the years. Since my own self-worth had taken such a hit with my being fired, I was especially intrigued by a certain passage in his book, beginning with the first paragraph of his last chapter:

Two hours before, I had sauntered into the dingy little secondhand bookshop in one of the side streets of the Loop. Depressed and heavyhearted at the thought of a great personal defeat I had just sustained to one of my life's ambitions, I wandered aimlessly among the counters stacked high with bargains in books. At one of the tables I tumbled over dusty volume after volume, glancing briefly at titles, flipping the pages of some that looked more promising, and browsing in others that mildly interested me. The shadows had already grown deeper in the canyon of the street that cowered under Chicago's skyscrapers, and I decided I had almost outstayed my welcome. But then I picked up a thin little volume entitled *Courage* and began to read.

Soon my roving eye caught the lines of an old ballad, and two of its phrases gave me such a mental lift that I bought the book and was happy with my bargain.

Isn't it remarkable how inspiration has a way of arising sometimes out of the most unpromising places? My hands were soiled from handing so many dusty tomes, my brow was perspiring from the close and stuffy little shop, but my spirit was soaring somewhere in the blue above the bustle of State Street. For in James M. Barrie's little volume I had found the formula for new resolves and increased effort.[7]

So what was the "great personal defeat" Tippet referenced? I set out to find the answer. Finally, I discovered what he was referring to. Tippett had dedicated many years of his busy life to the requirements involved in a doctoral degree, the most difficult of which was his doctoral dissertation, as he spent many years researching and writing it. Finally, on what was to be one of the high days of his life, he hand-carried it to the university, only to discover that some other scholar, somewhere in America, had beaten him to it. So all his long years of effort and travail had been in vain—and he was too old to start all over again. When I discovered *that*, I realized that

my getting fired paled compared to the devastating loss *he* had suffered. So, I set about seeking copies of his books for my own library. I was able to round up not only *Who Waits in Faith* (1951) but also books such as *My Lord and I* (1948), *Radiant Horizons* (1956), *Live Happier* (1957), *Key in Your Hand* (1964), and *The Voice from Sinai* (1964). They are *all* both powerful and insightful. The result is that a man I never had the opportunity to meet personally nevertheless has become one of my life's primary mentors. And through all the long years since that day, I have returned again and again to Tippett's insights into life.

It is safe to say that Milton Murray's morning with us turned out to be one of the key life-changing days of my lifetime. No small thanks to it, even after I discovered that I'd been fired under suspicious circumstances one day when the hospital president was on the road, I decided not to make an issue of it. I also decided to avoid at all costs getting bitter about it and badmouthing the hospital. The surprising result was that, upon being reminded by Milton Murray that it takes a minimum of three years for a new development director to establish credibility with donors [and I'd been fired without cause during my six-months probationary period], the hospital president became the chief advocate in helping me find a new position, telling prospective employers that "We didn't give Joe a chance—not half a chance—to show what he could do!"

Ironically, though I was subsequently hired on as development director of a large television ministry, I was fired again during my probationary period, also without cause; but by this time, no small thanks to Murray and Tippett, I'd hit my stride and was able to bridge back into the academic world, where I remained for ten years.

Which brings me to this conclusion: because of my hubris, bordering on arrogance, the Lord needed to take me to the woodshed twice before He felt comfortable with entrusting me with the greatest challenge of my lifetime: this all-consuming story ministry. Again and again, Tippett, in his books, points out that we are such a perverse species that we almost never grow during good times—only in trauma do we belatedly realize how much we need God, and thus grow. I can now, in retrospect, see that God had lessons to teach me that I could have learned in no other way than to leave the "safe" world of academia and twice suffer defeat where I was the proverbial "fish out of water" (professions I knew little about and in which I had no support system of people who might have aided me). In the crucible of those two years, I grew more than during any other time period of my life.

I now realize that, sooner or later, in life, God puts to use every detour, every dead end, every mistake, every humiliation, every misunderstanding, every discrediting, we have ever had to endure, in order to hammer us into shape for whatever challenges He has in store for us. *Nothing* is ever wasted with God: each zig and zag in our journey God anticipates and finds a place for in the story of our life.

I shall conclude with two Tippett quotations included in the introduction to my book *What's So Good About Tough Times?*

God knows that the things we acquire too easily are lightly esteemed. Perhaps that is the reason He hides many a blessing from us. He hides Himself, therefore, in pain that we may know His healing. He hides His best gifts in baffling disciplines, that they may come forth with the glow of the eternal. He conceals His purposes from His righteous Jobs, that they may reveal them to His pleading Jacobs. "The kingdom of heaven is like unto a treasure hid in a field," Jesus said. God designed that our possession of it should be a continual quest, even to the dedication of all that we have.[8]

And, as for compensation, I turned again to Tippett in that same introduction:

[God] brings the dawn out of the most dismal night. He makes our balmy springs and fruitful summers to succeed the bitter blasts of winter. Out of blustery, tempestuous March He makes way for our singing Aprils and our flowering Mays. Out of ten thousand storms He develops the giant redwood tree, and in the cloud forms His noblest symphony of color, the rainbow. Likewise out of forty years of banishment and obscurity God carved a Moses, out of cruel betrayal into the hands of aliens He molded the statesman Joseph; out of physical, mental, and spiritual suffering, He demonstrated the perfection of Job.[9]

1. Harry Moyle Tippett, *Who Waits in Faith* (Review and Herald® Publishing Association, 1951), 8.
2. Ibid., 9, 10.
3. Ibid., 10.
4. Ibid., 12.
5. Ibid., 120.
6. Ibid., 127.
7. Ibid., 119, 120.
8. Harry Moyle Tippett, *Who Waits in Faith* in *What's So Good About Tough Times?* (Waterbrook/Random House 2001), n.p.
9. Harry Moyle Tippett, *Live Happier* in *What's So Good About Tough Times?* (Waterbrook/Random House 2001), n.p.

*M*y paternal grandmother, Ruby Wheeler, was deaf—had been so since her late teens. As a result, her world—except for her husband—was small. She communicated with her grandchildren by reading lips. But her real world was her garden—and the flowers bloomed their hearts out for her. I've often wondered what her thoughts were there in the soundless world of her garden.

A Temperamental Garden

Faith Harris Leech

On a quiet, elm-bordered street of a certain southern city stood the ivy-covered brick house of Mr. Horton Lane, superintendent of the city schools. On this particular afternoon in early spring his eighteen-year-old daughter, Isabel, sat at the old-fashioned grand piano very languidly practicing her music. Her thoughts were really a block away, where a number of cars were drawn up before a large and imposing colonial residence. From the window she could see girls in soft, gay wraps step from limousines and electrics and hurry up the terraced walk to the house. She turned away and dropped into a deep, sagging easy chair, closing her eyes with a sigh of complete unhappiness. She wondered if she would ever grow used to this miserable ache of discontent.

Isabel had graduated from the high school the previous June, after four happy years, during which she had been very popular among her classmates. It had not occurred to her that after graduation, changes might come

in these associations. She knew that her father had only the most moderate income, with no margin to be spent by her in elaborate entertaining such as many of her classmates, daughters of wealthy men, were able to afford; but she was slow to believe that this fact would separate her from her friends. However, on this spring afternoon the climax seemed to be reached, as she watched the line of cars before the Lee mansion, and knew that Barbara was entertaining and had not invited her.

At breakfast the next morning, Mr. Lane looked up from his mail. "Anna," he said to his wife, with a deprecatory sigh, "I have a letter from that garden expert who is being sent here to lecture in the schools and start experimental gardens. Er—" he hesitated and looked so guilty that Mrs. Lane laughed.

"You are trying to muster courage to confess that you have already invited him to be our guest while he is in the city," she accused him.

Her husband grinned sheepishly. "Yes,

that is what I have done," he admitted, "and I had forgotten to tell you. This letter says he will be down the first of next week."

Monday evening found the Lanes listening with absorption while Mr. Edward Allison, garden expert, expounded upon the homely charms of cabbages and carrots and such things. . . . "My sister," he turned to Mrs. Lane, "has a splendid vegetable garden, and she does all the work in it herself. One year when she was feeling rather down, she started it just as a kind of diversion. She tells us now that she used to take her 'blues' and go out and plant them along with her radishes, and whenever she got into a temper she'd work it off pulling weeds out of the asparagus bed. She says the finest thing that garden has produced is a contented woman. Not a bad idea, don't you think?"

"Does your sister live in the country?" asked Isabel abruptly.

"No, in Washington," Mr. Allison answered. "She has turned her backyard into a garden. It is not much larger than my pocket handkerchief," he laughed, "but it produces about all the vegetables her small family needs."

The next morning, Isabel was returning from a lecture by the expert, delivered at the high school, when a large touring car filled with girls passed her. One of the occupants turned and nodded a careless greeting. Isabel

flushed and bit her lip to keep back her tears. It was Barbara Lee who had bowed—Barbara, who had been one of her very best friends in school, but who had paid her little or no attention since, so absorbed was she in her present social life, which had swept her away from all associations who weren't part of it.

Isabel went home with the old ache of loneliness. In her own room she took off her hat and stood staring moodily out across the neat backyard, wondering vaguely whether anybody was ever so miserable and discontented as she. Suddenly something Mr. Allison had said came into her mind. His sister had planted her "blues" along with her radishes. Isabel smiled faintly at the idea, and then, all at once, her eyes focused upon a small backyard, and the expression in them became bright and intent.

Late that afternoon, Mr. Lane was astonished to find his guest out in the rear yard deep in conversation with Isabel. "What in the world are they doing?" he demanded of his wife as they watched Mr. Allison stepping off certain measurements, which Isabel faithfully noted down on a piece of paper.

"Isabel has decided to plant a garden," Mrs. Lane explained, "and Mr. Allison is helping her lay it out."

A week later the backyard was a carefully plotted area, and Isabel was impatiently watching for those first tiny green tokens which would be the rewards of her labor. The first of May showed sturdy rows of English peas, firm little scarlet button radishes, tomato plants securely protected from heat and sudden spring chills, and many other plants promising a good harvest. Already the garden was receiving attention in the neighborhood, and Isabel's word about blights and bugs was accepted as authoritative. Mrs. Lane, watching the pretty gardener grow tan from outdoor work and absorbed in her venture, came to understand that the neat rectangular space was in reality a sort of battleground where Isabel was conquering unhappiness, and in the complete consolation of an occupation escaping from small envies and discontent.

The summer which came, with its great training camps and the paraphernalia of war and the consequent strain of hard times, was a terrible one to a people long accustomed to the precious monotony of peace and plenty. Everywhere organizations sprang up, formed to serve the country in some capacity. The middle of July, announcement was made that Mrs. B——, a woman known throughout the nation for her efficient service in the war zone, had returned to America to assist her country-women in directing their energies to the best ends for the public welfare. Isabel read that the Junior Service League of the city had invited Mrs. B—— to address them, and for the first time in a long while she felt a pang of her old unhappiness, for she knew that she would not have an opportunity of hearing the celebrity. The Junior Service League was made up entirely of the season's *debutantes* and their own intimate circle from which Isabel had long since disappeared.

But on a certain July afternoon, when all thoughts of the Junior Service League and Mrs. B—— had passed from Isabel's mind, and clad in khaki skirt and sport shirt, she was busily clearing out dried pea vines and bean stalks to make way for her fall garden, the maid came out with two cards. Isabel surveyed them at first indifferently and then with complete astonishment. The one read, "Miss Barbara Lee"; the other, "Mrs. Archibald B——."

When Isabel entered the sitting room, Barbara greeted her gushingly. "Isabel dear, this is Mrs. B——. I am sure I don't have to tell you who she is. She came down to lecture before the Junior Service League, and found us in a very bad way, I am afraid."

Hardly heeding Barbara's chatter, Isabel was looking into the fine dark eyes of the tall, prematurely gray-haired woman, who was returning her look with one of keen interest. "They tell me, Miss Lane," she observed abruptly, "that you have a garden which you have engineered entirely yourself."

"Yes," Isabel admitted, turning an inquiring glance upon Barbara, who laughed a little pettishly.

"Mrs. B——," she said, "found that the Junior Service League didn't know how to do much of anything except drive an automobile, and she didn't seem to think that a very vital thing to know. Finally, in desperation, we told her about your garden to divert her attention from our inefficiency. She wanted to come and see you and the garden right away."

"Has it been a practical success?" Mrs. B—— asked, after Barbara's explanation of their visit.

"My garden? Oh yes, distinctly so," Isabel replied. "I have kept books, you see. I know exactly what it has cost me and what my profits have been."

"Good!" Mrs. B—— exclaimed. "That is really businesslike. The maid said you were in your garden when we came."

"Yes," Isabel answered. "I am laying out my fall garden. With times as they are, I am planning to plant everything I can."

"Good!" Mrs. B—— exclaimed again, and turned to Barbara. "You see, Miss Lee, this young lady is doing something that is actually productive, that helps to solve one of our most difficult problems—that of the food supply. . . . How did you happen to go in for gardening, Miss Lane?"

Isabel looked embarrassed for a moment and then laughed. "I started my garden as a sort of graveyard for moods and 'blues' and that kind of thing, and then when it began to pay so well I became interested in it for its own sake."

Mrs. B—— nodded and smiled understandingly. The three of them spent a while in looking at the garden, and Mrs. B—— took her departure with the remark to Isabel: "The country needs girls like you, my dear."

The next Tuesday morning a letter came for Isabel, stating that the city had decided to open a garden department in the public schools, and offering her the position of demonstrator and lecturer, at a generous salary. The mayor stated that she had been most highly recommended for this position by the distinguished Mrs. B——.

"O Father, you are going to let me do it, aren't you?" pleaded Isabel with shining eyes.

"Of course, my dear," he said, and added with a laugh: "I'll turn over all my irritable teachers and incorrigible pupils to you, and you may make them plant themselves and see if they can come up as contented and happy as you are."

W*hat an epiphany! To realize for the first time that even the smallest of children are perfectly capable of understanding the deep things of God.*

One never knows how chance words we may casually say may affect those who hear them, not just on that day but for all time to come.

I've plenty of both kinds in my memory banks, to bless and burn, as I look back over the years: the ones when my lesser self took command and I said things that cut then, and never stopped cutting afterwards. And, fortunately, the other kind as well. But it's the cutting ones that have kept me awake at night.

This old story is one I'll guess you'll have just as hard a time forgetting as I have.

SOMETHING TO CARRY HOME

Author Unknown

The Sabbath School teacher was hot, tired, and irritable as she walked into the hot and stuffy church. Thus it was easy to lash out at Julia Simpson and her tiny brother, Eben.

As Eben left, he said, in his childish yet solemn way, "I'll be dood, and pray Dod."

And so it began.

Raising my parasol as I stepped out upon the front porch, I looked over the road which stretched out to the church, whose white spire rose above green trees in the distance, and wondered how I was to get over that hot hill, where not a shadow broke the glare. Such a sudden outpouring of the sun's heat seemed quite overpowering.

When I entered the church, I found my class of pupils nearly complete. I opened the closely shut window nearby, and dropped into my straight-backed chair, feeling as if there was not an atom of reserve force left in me

with which to tackle my duties. It was discouraging to have such feelings to contend with when I had striven so, but an hour ago, for a prayerful, tranquil mind; and I strove to overcome it. But the children, rubbing their feet on the bare floor, nearly set me wild, and I was glad when the opening bell called us to order. But I did not regain complete control of myself; for when, after the lesson was well begun, Julia Simpson came in, dragging by the hand such a little mite of a brother who seemed too small to be anywhere but at home, I was annoyed. *Why can't mothers be their own nurse girls?* I thought. And I'm afraid there was the least mite of sharpness in my voice as I said, "You should not bring such a baby to Sabbath School, Julia."

"Mother said I had got to stay and take care of him, then," was Julia's reply.

I made room for him and gave the little fellow a book of pictures to keep him from talking; but of course it wasn't a minute before the book went, with a bang, on the floor.

When this happened the third time, and just as I was saying, "Now, children," I took the book, and much to the child's apparent wonderment, heaved it onto the table. After this, for a while, the child was determined to do the talking himself; and of course every time he gave utterance to anything, in his funny baby fashion, a suppressed titter would break out from somewhere among the thirty-five children composing the class. But at last I seemed to get a little of the child's attention. I think it came from my talking of the verse, "His flesh shall be fresher than a child's" (Job 33:25, KJV) and calling the children's attention to how beautiful soft, rosy cheeks like Julia's little brother's were, and I took one of his chubby little hands, to show them the difference between such flesh and mine. At any rate, the latter part of the exercise the child sat crouched down in a sort of listening way, as if giving his undivided attention.

When we finished, and they went out, "Eben," as Julia called him, raised his great black eyes to mine, and said, in his slightly solemn, childish way, "I'll tome adain."

"Yes," I said, "and you must be a good little boy."

"I'll be dood, and pray Dod," he said, nodding his head like a wise judge, and marching away.

The last thing I had striven to impress upon the children's minds had been the need of prayer—for everything and at all times—and I was surprised that even so much, as seemed by the child's words, had been grasped by him.

And going home, thinking it over, I thought the breeze seemed a great deal fresher than when I had gone over the road before, though it was an hour nearer noon; and the way seemed not half so long and tiresome.

The next Sabbath I looked for little Eben, but Julia came without him, and in time the incident of his ever having come slipped from my mind.

A few weeks later I stood one morning out among my late roses, clipping and tying up, and smelling of this and that half-open rose, when a "hem" caused me to turn suddenly, and I found a woman standing beside me. How she had opened the gate and come up the gravel walk without my knowing it was a mystery; but there she was, and as she did not say anything, I said, "Good morning." She answered with a nod, and then stood awkwardly twisting the fringe of her shawl between her thumb and finger. Not knowing what else to say, I asked, "Can I do anything for you?"

"Well, no—that is, I only thought I'd like you to know we'd got on the right track again."

"Ah," I said, not having the remotest idea as to who "we" were or what the "track" was they had generally been on.

"Yes, I felt as if I'd like you to know how much good you'd done us."

"I!" I said in astonishment, as I pulled off my garden gloves and, walking to the porch, pushed one of the garden chairs toward my strange visitor, taking the remaining one myself. "I do not see how that can be when I have never seen you before."

"But you've seen Bub," and the woman laughed, and the laugh seemed to take ten years right off her life.

"Bub! Who's Bub?" I asked, struggling to get hold of what the woman was driving at.

"Why, my Bub, Ebenezer, that Julia took to Sabbath School."

"Oh," I said, the "Julia" letting in a little light. "You're Julia Simpson's mother? I remember little Eben's coming with her one day. Yes, yes."

"Well, you see,"—and the woman settled back, as if surer of her ground now,—"I used to mind about religion, quite a sight, when we were first married. But after things got to going so hard with us, and it was work, work, and money always short, and so little time for anything, we kinder forgot about it; and when we didn't, there didn't seem much chance for such things. And I used to tell Rufus—he's my husband—that there wasn't much time for poor folks to be religious in, and he seemed to think it was about so. Well, as I started to

say, a couple of days after Bubby went to Sabbath School was what some folks call a 'blue Monday.' The baby'd been worryin' all night."

"Eben?" I asked.

"Oh no; you hain't seen my baby yet. She's most a year old. As I was sayin', she'd kept me awake; and now there was the big washing, and the sun up so hot before I got at it; and taking it all together, it seemed as if I never could go through with it all. And after I'd groused a little, I dropped into a chair, sayin', 'It's no sort o' use; I *never* can do it.' Bub was on the floor with the baby's playthings, and I didn't suppose he was minding me one bit; but he looked up with those great eyes o' his'n, and says he:

" 'Why don't you tell Dod so?'

"I thought it must be I hadn't heard him right, and so I asked, 'What did you say, Eben?'

" 'I say,' rising to his feet, 'why don't you tell Dod so?'

"I got right up, and went about my work, but I was sort o' numb-like as if I'd got a blow. You see it was so queer-like for Eben to talk that way. I tried to move about lively, and get myself free, but I couldn't. At last I went into the bedroom, where baby was in bed asleep, and, shutting the door, I did just tell the Lord all about it, just how tired I was, and how hard everything was going, and how little strength I had, and asked Him to help me through the day—and when I went back to the kitchen my heart was as light as a feather, and I broke out singing as if I were a girl.

"But I hain't got to the best of it," she continued, as I moved a little to get my handkerchief. "If you'll believe me, as I was staking out the first boiling, who should come in but Rufus, and says he, 'I didn't have quite the right lumber I wanted for the job, so I thought it was so late I'd come home and help a bit, and not go after it till noon.' Now I don't believe Rufus had done such a thing as that afore since the first year we was married, and what do you suppose could have put it into his head, unless—"

Mrs. Simpson hesitated, *As if I might not quite agree with her*, I thought. So I hastened to say, "Unless the Lord put it into his heart? Of course you have a perfect right to think it is direct answer to prayer."

"Well, so it seemed to me and Rufus," said Mrs. Simpson, pulling her shawl up around her; "and you don't know what a comfort it has been to us, and we have just made a new start; and it's wonderful how easy things do go now. And when I went by this morning, and saw you a-standing' in the garden, I felt as if I'd like you to know what a sight of good what Bubby brought did for us." And with another shake of her head she walked away.

After she had gone I felt a good deal as if I ought to ask somebody's pardon; and I went down before God, in that little back parlor of mine, for a long time; and the next Sabbath, when Julia brought in Eben, gay in his new suit of blue waterproof, with brass buttons, I gave him the very best seat there was; and all that lesson time I tried to strip my talk free from big words, so that even the smallest should have something to carry home.

*T*here are two kinds of tragedies," declared Aunt Jane: "the quick kind—and the slow kind." Lois grieved for the first kind—but it took her a while before she realized how close she was to the second kind.

It is all too easy to take people for granted, especially *those closest to us. I know all too well: were my father still alive today, I'd reassure him again and again of how much I appreciate all he has meant to us through the years.*

Two Kinds of Tragedy

Author Unknown

"O Aunt Jane, did Mother tell you what a terrible thing happened this morning?" Lois Martin asked, as she met her aunt coming down the walk as she was going in, late in the afternoon.

"About the Graydon girl's mother? Yes, she told me," Aunt Jane answered briefly.

"I never heard of anything so terribly sad," Lois said, with a quiver in her voice. "Marjorie Graydon and her mother were so perfectly congenial, just like chums, and for her to be killed instantly in that wreck, so soon after she had said good-bye to Marjorie, seemed too terrible for words. Marjorie was telling us, just after her mother had started for home, what a perfectly lovely summer they had had together. We girls have just been so distraught we couldn't study all day. It is the first time I ever had a tragedy come so near me."

Aunt Jane looked at her niece grimly. "There are tragedies and tragedies," she said. "I've seen the quick kind, and I've seen the slow kind, and if you're killed, you're killed, I guess, whichever kind it is.

"The slow kind is mostly where people are giving up their whole lives for others who are too blind to appreciate their efforts, or ever say, 'Thank you,' or a kind word.

"I've never been a mother, but it seems to me that if I had been, and if I'd been given my choice of a death, I should rather have gone like the Graydon girl's mother than like some I've seen. They had had their good times together, you say, and so, not having any bitter regrets, the Graydon girl can get over her sorrow after a while, and she'll always have the last lovely summer to remember. Yes, there are quick tragedies and slow ones, but when a mother's gone, she's gone."

Aunt Jane turned, and went down the street toward her home. Looking after her, Lois said, half to herself: "Aunt Jane is so queer. She didn't seem one bit sympathetic over poor Marjorie's trouble."

Lois went through the library, sitting room, and dining room in search of her mother. Out on the kitchen table she found the pretty dish of salad and the roll of pressed meat which she had promised and her mother had prepared for the spread which was to follow the party that evening. On the rack in the dining room was the weekly ironing, and the greater part of it was the fluffy summer apparel belonging to Lois. The beautifully ironed white dress which she was to wear the next afternoon always required an hour of mother's skillful work, and Lois wondered casually how she ever accomplished so much in a day. She went on up to the sewing room, where her mother was putting the finishing work on a filmy party frock, which Lois was to wear that evening.

She was running the narrow ribbons through yards and yards of dainty lace beading. Something in the tired droop of the slender figure and the wistful look in the eyes, as she glanced up with her usual cheery smile, gave thoughtless Lois a curious shock. What if the tragedy had come to her instead of Marjorie! What could she ever do without her mother! Then Aunt Jane's words seemed to ring in her ears: "There are quick tragedies and slow ones, but when a mother's gone, she's gone."

Lois took the dress from her mother's hands, saying, "You are going right downstairs this minute, and you're going to lie on the couch and rest until Father comes home to supper."

"But you wanted your dress for tonight, and there are yards of ribbon to run yet," her mother objected weakly.

"Yes, and I know who will run them," Lois answered. "And I've plenty of time to get supper, too, before Father comes. I'll take the dress downstairs and sit right by you, to see that you lie still."

Mrs. Martin lay quite still, watching Lois with loving eyes, wondering what had made her daughter suddenly thoughtful of her comfort; but she understood a little later when Lois had finished the dress and started to prepare the supper, then came back, and dropping down beside the couch, threw both strong young arms about her mother and clasped her close, as if she could never let her go, and said, in a choked whisper, "O Mother, dear, what if it had happened to me, instead of Marjorie!"

And as Lois went about her work, she whispered over and over, pleadingly, "If You'll only spare her to me, I'll be more thoughtful." And the One for whom the whispered words were intended must have heard and granted her request, for Lois Martin and her mother have had a number of summers together since that day—lovely summers that can be remembered without any bitter regrets.

*N*ever before had I come across a story characterized by four *epiphanies. It is such a remarkable letter from a father to his son that it was published in the pages of* American Magazine *before* The Youth's Instructor *picked it up.*

WHEN SUCCESS HUNG IN THE BALANCE

A Father

The truly great life cannot be measured by financial standards. Some of the most worthy lives have always been conscious of the stings of poverty. But the principles outlined in the following letter, written by a father to his son, have their bearing in every true life, whether it be counted a monetary success or failure. One must be persistent, must keep everlastingly at one's task, and must be continually pressing toward the mark of a high goal if he would attain true success in either the religious or the business world. As you read the letter you will discover that each of the foundation stones upon which this father's successful career was built characterizes every other real success. Unfortunately the son to whom the letter was addressed died before the father, so the letter, which was not to be opened until after the father's death, failed of its original purpose. But the executors have given it to the press that the sons of other fathers may profit by it. The letter follows as it appeared in the *American Magazine*.

"My Dear Boy: Miss Farson has just put a desk calendar for the new year in front of me. Every year, on the day before Christmas, she has it ready, and every year I turn over the leaves after she has left the office at night, and make a little private mark of my own against four dates.

"I call them my 'crossroads days.'

"Among the men in our line of business I am regarded as a fair success. I suppose if I were to close out tomorrow and retire, I should have two hundred thousand in the box where you will find this letter. That isn't a fortune according to the standards of today; but when you remember that I started with nothing, it isn't a bad showing for twenty-five years of active work.

"Not that I consider money the most important thing in life. It isn't. But money, after all, is stored-up human energy. It's the part of your life that hasn't slipped away from you. These two hundred thousand dollars represent the energy of twenty-five years of my life, plus little particles from hundreds of other lives that have worked for me. They will give back to me or to you just as much energy as has been put into them. They will support me for another twenty-five years; they will buy for me the lives of twenty-five other men. Just as coal is compressed, stored-up sunshine, so money is human energy, human life in stored-up form. That's why it plays so large a part in our affairs; why, in a sense, we use it as a measure of success.

"But that is by the side. I was saying to you that men call me a success. Yet, looking back over my life, I realize that on four different days in my life I stood at the crossroads between success and failure, and on two of them narrowly missed the wrong road. These are my crossroads days:

April 16, 1883.
September 2, 1887.
January 5, 1891.
October 29, 1901.

"You will receive much advice from older men on how to succeed. It would be of more help to you if they would take you into their inside offices and tell you frankly how they almost failed. For I am convinced that the road to success in every man's life runs very close to the precipice of failure; that there are days when it is saved not so much by his own wisdom or virtue as by some lucky turn of the scales. Most men are not honest enough to confess it; they prefer to forget such days. I prefer to remember them, and I want you to know their story; for you are my only son. There is no chamber of my heart that I would keep closed from you if by opening it I could help you even a little bit when you come to your own crossroads days.

"April 16, 1883: The Day When I Found Myself

"You do not remember your grandfather; you were only three years old when he died. He was a good father, but never demonstrative. I sometimes felt almost sorry for him. He had a reputation for being cold and austere, whereas he was, in fact, warmhearted, sympathetic, and really a little timid underneath. Nature seemed to have left out of his makeup any facility in signaling his emotions to the outside world. He was a soul shut up within himself; and I know now that he must have been often hungry for understanding and companionship. Yet the world called him cold; and we children thought he did not love us.

"I, too, grew up close-mouthed, shrinking, timid, yearning for friendship, yet afraid to go halfway on the road in search of it. Yet, in justice to him, he gave me rich endowments also. One of these was the habit of incessant work;

another was hatred of a lie; and another was a college education.

"As I write this, at the age of fifty-nine, I am in almost perfect health. I sleep well; my color is fine; I do my work easily, and without more than the normal amount of fatigue. You have heard men envy me my good health. Yet there is hardly one of them who did not have a far better start than I. For the first twenty-four years of my life I hardly knew what it was to have a day free from pain. I was nervous, depressed, afflicted with hours of the blackest despondency. If I am well today, and apparently good for another twenty years, it is because I have *worked* for good health; any other man, I am convinced, could have done what I have done if he had fought as steadily and as long.

"I matured very little in college. I came out weak, nervous, with no idea as to how or where I should find a place. My father gave me the benefit of the doubt for two weeks, and then, discovering that I had no definite ideas of any kind, sent me to a friend of his, the president of the bank at Easthaven. I went, feeling his critical, disappointed glance upon me; determined to hold my job and change his opinion, even though it killed me.

"At the end of three months I was home again, in disgrace. Two other positions my father obtained for me in quick succession. In one I lasted six months; in the other, six weeks.

When my third employer called me into his office and told me, not unkindly, that I was entirely unsuited to the work I was trying to do and might as well quit, I held myself together until I was out of sight of the office, and then I threw my arm across my face and dropped onto a park bench and cried.

"I was a failure, my boy; I had been given a college education; thousands had been spent in fitting me for life, and there was no place in life for me. The men who were in college with me had found their niches: they had settled down. Some of them were already so sure enough of themselves that they had married and established homes. And here I was, almost a year after my graduation, a failure in three different positions, nervously worn out, apparently a cumberer of the earth.

"All the night long I sat on that bench fighting a battle for life. Yes, actually a battle for life; for my first impulse was to end the whole miserable business. I had had my chance. I was unfit to survive. *Let me, then, take myself out of the way and leave room for those who had proved their right to it.* Along toward morning, with the first faint rays of light in the east, light came into my torn soul. I made up my mind that, failure though I might be, I would not add cowardice to my sins. My parents were ashamed of me, and rightly; but I would not plunge them into the final shame. 'There is something in the world

I can do,' I said to myself. 'I believe that I could earn my living as a carpenter.' Queer idea, it may seem to you. I suppose it came because carpentry was in such sharp contrast to the jobs in which I had failed.

"That morning I walked to the post office, sent a brief note to my father, and took a train to this city. If there had been a carpenter shop near the depot, or a shop offering manual labor of any sort, I should have walked in. Instead, some kinder fate led me past the office of the *News,* and there on the bulletin board was a rough sign: 'Strong boy wanted.' Fifteen minutes later I had convinced the janitor of the building that I was qualified for the work he wanted done; and at the end of the week I went home with five dollars in my pocket. Poor pay, but I had earned it, and the gruff old fellow had said a kind word to me as he handed it over. *I had made good at something!* There was a thrill in that which compensated for the smelly room where I lodged, and the weary muscles and the miserable food.

"I had always wanted to write, and after a time I began slipping an item now and then onto the city editor's desk. Within three months I had a place on the city staff. There, with the smell of printer's ink in my nostrils and the roar of the presses under my feet, I found my place in the world—the job I could do, and be happy while doing.

"The job on the *News* came in the summer of 1883; but the day I celebrate came three months earlier, April 16. On that day I stood on the crossroads a failure—and I refused to admit that I was a failure. On that day I found myself.

"It may be—I hope it will be—that I shall live to see you out of college and through that difficult period of transition that follows. I know what boys suffer in the struggle to find their place in the world. I think I should know how to be more sympathetic and helpful than my father was. But in case I should not live that long, in case you come out of college to face the world alone, then I want you to re-read this record of my experience and take courage.

"Know that almost every young man who has amounted to anything in the world went through a period of bitter self-doubt and despondency. Read these words, written by one young man:

"What madness impels me to desire my own destruction? Why, forsooth, am I in the world? Since death must come to me, why should it not be as well to kill myself? If I were sixty years old or more I would respect the prejudices of my contemporaries and wait patiently for nature to finish her course; but since I began life in suffering misfortune and nothing gives me pleasure, why should I endure these days, when nothing I am concerned in prospers?

"Who was he? you ask. What weakling, what utter failure, was this? His name became well known only a few years after those words were written. It was Napoleon Bonaparte.

"When Lincoln was thirty-two, and life seemed to promise little more than a law practice in rural Illinois, he wrote to his partner, Stuart:

"I am now the most miserable man living. If what I feel were equally distributed to the whole human family there would not be one cheerful face on earth. Whether I shall ever be better I cannot tell. I awfully forbode I shall not. To remain as I am is quite impossible. I must die to do better, it appears to me . . . I can write no more.

"I want you to know, my boy, if you, too, must go through days of bitterness before you find your place in the world, that your experience will not be unique. And you will conquer. You will conquer because you have the right blood in your veins, and the right chin—and because your father conquered before you.

"September 2, 1887: The Day I Became Dependable

"The first six months of work on the *News* gave me what I still lacked in self-assurance. I knew that I had found my place in the world; I was confident I could hold it against all comers. Indeed, I became almost too confident. I hadn't been working six months before I received an offer to go over to the *Journal*. And from that time on, if six months went by without an offer of some sort I began to think there was something the matter with me. Our business, as you know, is peculiarly one of ideas; it is almost as fluid as ideas themselves. The temptation to flow about in it from job to job, selling your ideas in each new job at a slightly larger figure is very great. In the years between twenty-three and twenty-seven I changed jobs no less than seven times. And finally, on my twenty-seventh birthday, I walked into my employer's office and handed in my resignation.

" 'Why, Bert!' he exclaimed, 'What's the matter? I didn't know you were dissatisfied.'

" 'Not dissatisfied,' I answered.

" 'Well, what's the idea, then?'

" 'Tired of working,' I said. 'I'm just going to quit because I'm going to quit, that's all. I'm young, Mr. Sartwell, and I'm only going to live once. Therefore I'm going to enjoy myself all I can. You work all the time, harder than I do, and yet you own the business and are rich. That may be your idea of a good newspaperman; I can get my fifty a week any time I want to go after it. I wanted to work long enough to prove that I could make good. Now I'm going to quit for a while. I'm going around the world.'

" 'H'm,' he mused. 'Going alone?'

" 'No. Anderson's going with me.'

"At that his jaw dropped. Anderson and I were the two best men on his staff. He reached forward and shook his finger under my nose.

" 'Bert,' he said, speaking very slowly and impressively, 'I've always made it a rule in business to accept resignations, and I'm going to accept yours. But I'm going to tell you something, and you can pass it on to Anderson with my compliments. You two young fellows are in the most dangerous position of any two young men I know. You have ability, too much ability. If you had only a little, so that you had to sit tight and plug every minute, you'd be fairly safe. You'd move along up in business slowly, but surely, as the fellows ahead of you died off. But you two are brilliant. It's true you can get your fifty a week whenever you want it. And that's your danger. You will go rolling around collecting fifty a week here and fifty a week there, and you'll never stay long enough in one place to get seventy-five a week, or a hundred a week. Or two hundred a week. Oh, I know your type! You may not give me credit for much sense now, but

when I was your age I was exactly in your fix. And I want to tell you that if I hadn't taken myself by the neck and forced myself to stay put, I'd still be collecting fifty a week as a reporter instead of pulling down thirty-one thousand, as I did last year. With just your brilliance, and no stability, you're worth just about fifty a week. But it takes more than brilliance to be worth a really big job.'

"I shook hands with him, without replying. *He was just sore*, I thought, *because Anderson and I were leaving at once.* We chuckled over the interview on our way to New York. And in New York, at my college roommate's house, I met a friend of his sister's. Your mother can tell you what happened in the next two weeks. Sometime—perhaps when you meet your girl—she will tell you. But the upshot of it was that I deserted Anderson, spent on a diamond ring all the money that was to start us around the world, and a month from the day I had left the Old Man I was back in his office again.

" 'I've got stability, sir,' I said.

"He made no special comment—just told me to go back to my job. But I knew that from that moment he was keeping his eye on me. And from that day I began to move up.

"It wasn't until ten years later that I realized how important was the crossroads at which I stood on September 2, 1887, the day I met your mother. Ten years later I was sitting in my office after luncheon when the boy brought in a scrap of paper with a name scribbled on it. The name was Newton Anderson. He had taken his trip around the world; he had followed our youthful ideal of working only when he wanted to and throwing his jobs when they had lost their first thrill. And he was back in my office looking for work, for the same kind of work he had been doing ten years before, and the same pay—or less.

"Anderson was one of the most brilliant men who ever passed through the newspaper offices of this city. I stood with him at the crossroads. He took one road and I took the other. He continued to roam. I discovered that life is not a sprint but a marathon, that the best prizes come only to those who combine with their ability a power to keep everlastingly at it.

"Men have spoken to me admiringly of my 'persistence,' my ability to stick to a thing until it is finished. I accept their praise; it pleases me. Yet when I think of poor Anderson, I know that I don't really deserve any praise. If I had slept downtown with him on the night of September 2, 1887, instead of going uptown to my roommate's home, I shouldn't have met your mother. I shouldn't have gone back to work. I might be today where Anderson is—a rewrite man on the *Tribune* at thirty-five dollars a week. That was my second crossroads. You, too, will come to

it some day, my boy, when some petty irritation with the job will tempt you to toss it up. Remember, then, that nothing worthwhile is accomplished in this world except by men whom the world knows to be dependable. And, remembering that, you will go back to the job and conquer it, just as your father did.

"January 5, 1891: The Day I Got My Second Wind

"From the day when your mother said yes, I began to forge ahead in the office of the *News*. Every New Year's Day the Old Man would call me into his office, grunt his satisfaction, and raise my salary a little. I was tremendously happy in my work. Your mother and I had bought our little home in Edgemere, and were paying for it a little at a time. You and your sister had come to us. I was getting forty-five hundred dollars, enough to live well in Edgemere, and to give us something tucked away in the bank every year. For the first time in my life I was perfectly satisfied. My path seemed to stretch out straight and clear before me. A little more responsibility every year, a little more salary, no cause for worry or restlessness. Just solid, lasting content.

"That was my frame of mind on Christmas Day in 1890. Then New Year's came along and for the first time there was no summons to the front office, no raise in pay. 'The Old Man is busy,' I said to your mother that night.

'He has forgotten; he'll call me in a day or two.' But by the time January 5 came around with no message from him, I knew that he hadn't forgotten. I knew that for some reason he didn't intend to boost me that year at all.

"January 5 is my birthday. I pulled down my desk at three o'clock that day, and started out into the cold to walk the sixteen miles to Edgemere. I wanted to be alone; I needed to think. On that long walk home I ran over in my mind my own career to date, and the careers of all the other men whom I knew and had watched from year to year. I was looking for a hole. I wanted to know wherein I had failed. And about halfway out to Edgemere I hit upon the truth. . . .

"Running over the lives of the men I had known in business, I discovered this curious fact: Around thirty or thirty-five their careers began unmistakably to divide into two classes. Most of them had given promise of success; they had moved along about as I had until they had reached an income of four or five thousand dollars. There, half of them had stopped; the other half seemed to take a fresh grip on themselves and forge ahead even more rapidly. Why had the first group stopped?

"It wasn't lack of ability. So far as I could see, the men in the two groups did not differ greatly in talent; nor was it lack of opportunity. It was nothing more nor less than this— the first group had become satisfied: familiarity with their jobs had bred contentment, and contempt. They had settled down in suburbs, just as I had; they were happy with their children; their jobs were easy for them; they were at peace with the world; they had ceased to struggle, which means that they had ceased to grow.

"There is an old fable, my boy, which every business man ought to read. It tells of the birth of an heir to a certain king; and at his birth eleven fairies came, each bringing a gift. One brought beauty; one, charm; one, health; and so on. Finally a twelfth fairy appeared and tendered her gift. It was discontent. The king was very angry with the twelfth fairy, thinking that she mocked him. So he spurned the gift, and the fairy withdrew it. The little prince grew up; he was healthy, charming, good to look upon; but somehow he never made any progress, he never accomplished anything really worthwhile. He had lost the gift that would have been worth more to him than all the others combined—a divine discontent.

"I have heard of a big industrial concern that increased the salary of its general manager to $75,000 a year. The general manager was delighted; he thanked the board of directors. Now, he said to them, he had achieved his ambition—he was entirely satisfied. Within a year the president of that company had found a way to eliminate that man from the business.

'I want no man in my business,' he said, 'who is entirely satisfied.'

"That was my trouble. It was not because I was inefficient that no raise came to me on January 1, 1891. It was because I had let myself become satisfied. I had dropped into the habit of thinking of myself as a forty-five-hundred-dollar man, when I ought to have kept my estimate of myself always five thousand dollars above my salary.

"Before I reached home that afternoon, I had laid down a little program for myself. Here it is:

"*Program drawn up on my thirtieth birthday*

" '1. *Resolved*: That my income at fifty years of age is to be $25,000 a year.

" '2. *Resolved*: To attain this it will be necessary to meet the following budget:

> Income at 30 $4,500
> Income at 31 $6,000
> Income at 35 $8,000
> Income at 40 $15,000
> Income at 45 $20,000

" '3. No one can prevent me from meeting this budget: no one can stop my growth except myself.

" '4. And, further, I resolve to lay out for myself at once a course of reading which will tend to broaden me (the course to comprise not less than two new books a week) so that when I come to own a newspaper of my own, I shall be a really big editor, not merely a mediocrity.'

"You notice, my boy, that I didn't put any $5,000 mark on my budget. I have had a sort of superstitious horror of the $5,000 mark. So many men get up to $5,000 and stick there: they get themselves classed as $5,000 men, and are never able to outgrow the tag. I made up my mind to jump clear over the $5,000 mark—because once you have done that, the next stopping place is $10,000, and by that time a man ought to be going strong enough that he can't be stopped.

"Beware of the day when you will say to yourself: 'I know all there is to know about my job; it is a good job; I am content.' Gladstone took up a new language when past seventy. Titian died at ninety-nine, still painting and studying art. 'What we know is nothing; what we have to learn is everything' cried La Place, the astronomer, as he passed out at seventy-eight. Lay out a growing program for yourself, and measure yourself by it from year to year. Beware of the breathing spell that comes after the first period of success. That is the day when you will determine whether you are to be a really big man or only a fairly big man—the day when you get your second wind.

"October 29, 1901: The Day When I Met My Big Temptation

"We hear a great deal about the tragedies of youth. I am not afraid of any failure for you in youth. You will have your share of boyish follies; but you have a firm chin and a clean heart, and you will come through. It is in middle life that the really big tragedies come—when men of fine promise slip back into fatness; when covetousness eats away early ideals; when a man learns his price.

"It has been a dream with me, my boy, that someday I might be governor of my state. I have never confessed it to anyone, not even to your mother. A good many governors have come out of newspaper offices in recent years; why shouldn't the chance come to me? Two years ago it did come. The governorship was offered to me by the only authority that can offer it in this state,—Senator Harper,—and I accepted. For twelve hours I was as good as elected governor; the next morning at seven o'clock I withdrew.

"It was immediately after the *News* had come under my control. The Old Man had kept the *News* 'independent' in politics, which means that he had flattered both parties and been careful not to offend anyone. Senator Harper sent for me. I knew what he wanted. It was a crucial year. A fusion of reformers was attacking the old-line leaders. The senator did not expect me to make a party organ of the *News,* but he did hope to get the weight of its influence thrown in his favor for the coming campaign.

"And he promised me the governorship.

"I accepted, my boy. I went home happy.

My life's ambition was about to be realized. If my conscience pricked me a little, I silenced it. 'I was not selling myself,' I said. I hadn't agreed to support any dishonest men or measures. All I had agreed to do was not to support a movement which—while I agreed with many of its principles—was greatly marred by the ultraradicals within its ranks.

"So I argued. But while I was walking up and down in my study, fighting it out, you came in, my boy. And your sister came in, and your mother. And when I looked at you, it came over me all of a sudden what I had agreed to do. I knew what Harper's rule meant to our state. I knew the rotten deals he and his crowd had put over. I knew he had grown rich in office, and why he had grown rich, and how many thousands of families like ours had been mulcted to make him rich. . . .

"I could hardly wait for morning to come. I went to Harper's hotel before he was out of bed. I insisted on being shown to his room at once.

"It was a stormy interview; but when it was over, I felt like a new man. Every man, they say, has his price. I sometimes think the saying is true. Doubtless, I, too, have mine. But I thank God that so far no one has ever bid it. Thank God it is not a paltry price; not so paltry, at least, as the governorship.

"I have just looked at my watch. It is eleven o'clock. I have been writing to you almost five hours. It's a much longer letter than I meant to write; but these old memories, once you release them, flow out and take control of the pen. When, after I am gone, you find this letter, take your desk calendar and mark these four dates, and when they come around, boy, celebrate them a little as I used to do.

"April 16—the day I found my place in the world, after a year of bitter struggle and doubt.

"September 2—the day I began really to make progress.

"January 5—the day on which I got my second wind.

"October 29—the day I learned that it doesn't make much difference whether you live in a cottage or the governor's mansion. You still must live with yourself.

"The mind is its own place, and itself
Can make a heaven of hell, a hell of
heaven.

"You, too, will have your crossroads days, my boy. We all do. And when they come, may they be made a little easier for you by this letter from your affectionate old dad."

When we are young, all too often we speak or act first, and think second. Native Americans have a saying to the effect that we should not criticize anyone until we have first walked a day in his moccasins. How grateful I am personally, when something I've written that should never have been mailed—isn't.

POLLY HASTINGS' VALENTINE

Author Unknown

"Hal Prescott, you are a born artist, and no mistake! That's old Polly Hastings complete, only a little more so. But really you are not going to send it?"

"Send it? Of course I shall send it. We boys have owed the amiable Miss Polly a grudge for this many a day, and now we are going to pay it. She shall have a chance at last to see herself as others see her—cross, disagreeable old thing that she is. And Fred Raynor has written some comical rhymes to go with it."

"Very good, Hal! You and Fred had better go into the valentine business. You might make your fortunes. But, after all, isn't it most too bad to send that? Miss Polly isn't to blame for her looks, you know."

"Of course she isn't. Who said she was?" replied Harry, with some asperity. "But she can help her actions. Maybe she has never ordered you off her doorstep, or given you a calling down just because you happened to drop

a peanut shell or two on her sidewalk. And maybe she never sent you sprawling in the gutter, just as you were about to make your best bow to some young ladies."

"No, I have no such grievances as that to complain of or avenge," said Phil Graves, laughing. "But don't be too hard on the old lady, Hal. She has her troubles, I dare say; and maybe they don't improve her disposition."

St. Valentine's Day came, laden, as usual, with missives. Little Rose Prescott had been thoroughly happy all day. Several valentines had fallen to her share—all beauties; and as she sat in the fire-lighted parlor after supper, with her treasures in her hand, she wondered why every one should not agree with her that St. Valentine's was the most delightful day of the whole year, Christmas scarcely excepted.

But Harry was heartily tired of hearing of valentines, and of thinking about them, too; for, after all, his own exploit was not so agreeable to reflect upon as he had thought it would be, and he could not help questioning in his own mind if his behavior had been such as his conscience could approve. Therefore it was a relief to him when lights were dimmed and his father expressed his readiness to respond to the children's clamor for a story.

Rose begged for a valentine story; but Charlie wanted to hear how Grandpa's house burned down when Papa was a little boy no larger than himself. So Mr. Prescott began:

"I think it was in March that it happened, and a cold, windy night it was. Father had been suddenly called from home, and Mother was just recovering from a long and severe illness. How well I remember Father's leave-taking that day. I wanted to go with him, as I usually did, for I was the youngest boy, and a favorite with him. But this time it was not to be thought of, and Father was in too much haste to discuss the matter with me. 'Amanda,' said he, turning to an old woman who was Mother's special attendant, 'take good care of your mistress, and don't let these children disturb her. And, Polly,' turning to the young, rosy-cheeked nurse girl, 'I leave the little folks all in your hands, and shall feel sure that they are well cared for. Good-bye all!' And in a moment more Father was half-way to the gate.

"Somehow, as night came on, it was very lonely without Father; and when we were all seated around the great open fireplace, listening to the wild wind outside, it did not seem

as pleasant as usual. When eight o'clock came, we pleaded to sit up a little longer. But Polly knew Father's wishes in that matter too well to allow it, much as she might have wished it on her own account. Cousin Tim Arnold had come over to spend the night with George, who was usually my bedfellow; so it was decided to put me by myself in a small room at the head of the front stairs, commonly called the 'hall bedroom.'

"How long I slept I am unable to say. It may have been moments, or it may have been hours; but I was suddenly awakened by a sound like the fall of some heavy body, accompanied with a scream, and as I started up in bewilderment, my ears seemed filled with a rushing, crackling sound, quite unlike the roaring of the wind, and my room was so light that every object could be readily distinguished. My first emotion was that of fear; but second thought convinced me that morning had come, and springing from my bed, I commenced dressing, when suddenly a volume of smoke burst into the room, so strangling and bewildering me that I fell to the floor unconscious."

"Was the house afire, Papa?" asked Charley, eagerly.

"Yes, children, the house was on fire. It was so old and dry it seemed to burn like paper, and the wild wind, as it whistled and shrieked around the gables and among the tall chimneys, only helped on the mad fury of the flames, making the work of destruction more rapid and sure.

"The half-crazed servant girls ran from room to room, in helpless terror, dragging the sleeping children from their beds and carrying them to a place of safety. And poor sick Mother, in her helplessness, wrung her hands in agony and prayed to be left until every child had been safely removed from the burning house; and it was only when assured of their safety that she would consent to be borne away by the kind hands which had come to her rescue.

" 'They're all right, Mrs. Prescott; every one of 'em!' said a kindhearted farmer, who had assisted in her removal. 'Seven of 'em— four boys and three girls. We counted 'em, my wife and I, both of us.'

"Yes, the children had been counted a dozen times, at least; but Polly, to make the matter sure beyond a doubt, proceeded to number them once more. 'Tim Arnold!' she fairly shrieked, 'are you here? Then where is—oh! where is Jamie? Help! help!' shrieked Polly, as she fairly flew back to the burning house. 'Jamie is in the hall bedroom! Who will save him?'

"Two or three men started forward, but shrank back appalled, and, remembering their own wives and little ones at home, refused to brave the danger.

" 'Will no one go? Will no one save my Jamie?' cried the poor girl, wringing her hands. 'O Jamie, Jamie, you were left to my care!' Then seizing a blanket and throwing it about her own person, the heroic girl sprang past the hands that would have tried to stay her steps from what seemed certain death, rushed into the house, flew up the burning staircase, burst into the room where I was lying, and, in less time than it takes me to tell it, had taken my unconscious form in her arms, wrapped the blanket about me, and retraced her steps down the fiery path and out into the open air, just as the burning staircase fell behind us.

"Aid was not wanting to relieve her of my heavy weight, as she appeared, and eager hands snatched off the burning blanket. But the exertion had been too much for her strength; and burned by the fire and bewildered by the smoke, she had scarcely passed over the threshold, when she fell headlong, striking with her face an iron scraper, which inflicted a frightful wound."

"And was she very badly hurt, Papa?" asked Rose, with her eyes full of tears.

"Yes, my dear, Polly was badly hurt and sadly disfigured. It was many months before she recovered from her wound, her burns, and the dreadful shock to her nervous system. Indeed, she never again seemed like the joyous, light-hearted girl that she was before."

"I hope Grandpa rewarded her as she deserved," said Harry.

"It was hardly possible to do that," replied Mr. Prescott, "as she had rendered us a service for which money could not pay. But Father did what he could. We wished very much to give her a good education, as she was both anxious and quick to learn; but Providence saw fit to interfere. Her mother's death, which occurred soon after our house was burned, left to her care an imbecile father and a young brother; and no amount of persuasion could induce her to leave them to other hands, as she had promised her dying mother to care for both. So she gave up the best years of her life to her helpless parent, refusing at least two good offers of marriage on his account; and since his death she has had little chance for comfort or happiness, owing to the bad conduct of her brother, who has grown from a bright, beautiful, though sadly indulged little boy into a wicked profligate, who squanders her money and leads her a most wretched life. She says she cannot cast him off, as he was a legacy left by her precious mother. And she feels, too, that perhaps her too-indulgent training has helped to make him what he is. So she bears with him, endures his abuse, and pays his debts. Is it any wonder, children, if, under all these trials, her disposition has become soured, and all the sweetness seems to have been crushed out of her nature? Many people there are who think her morose and ill-tempered, and there are but few who know what a good, noble, unselfish heart Polly Hastings has under it all."

"Polly Hastings!" exclaimed Harry, starting to his feet and coloring to the roots of his hair.

"Polly Hastings!" repeated Charley. "What! That cross old woman who keeps a little fancy store on D— street?"

"The very same," said Mr. Prescott. "And now that you know that to her your father owes his life, perhaps you will try to be kind to her and speak pleasantly to her now and then."

"Oh! we will," exclaimed Rose.

"Of course we will," said Charley. "That is, if she'll give us a chance."

But Harry said nothing. With a heart full of grief, shame, and mortification, he sat with his bowed head resting upon his hand; and later in the evening, when he entered his father's library and poured out a full confession of his wrongdoing, Mr. Prescott knew that Harry was thoroughly penitent and had been sufficiently punished.

"I am glad, Harry," said his father, "that you are sorry for what you have done. But, my dear boy, I want you to realize that it is not only because Polly Hastings once saved your father's life that you should regret your conduct; for even if she were no more to us than any other person, you should always treat her with respect. As it is, you and Fred have not only insulted a woman, but have treated gray hairs with contempt."

"I know it, Father," replied Harry, with the deepest humility. "And I'm sure I don't know what we can do to atone."

"Fortunately, Harry, I have it in my power to help you out of your trouble, to some extent," said Mr. Prescott, smiling, and laying before Harry's astonished eyes his own caricature of Miss Polly.

"Why, Father!" exclaimed Harry. "How—where under the sun—"

"I discovered what you were about, my boy, in time to prevent this from being sent; and tonight, instead of being grieved and angry over the foolish conduct of two thoughtless boys, Miss Polly is rejoicing over a new fifty-dollar greenback from her devoted valentine."

"O Father, how glad, how relieved I am! And how can I thank you enough?"

"By proving to me, Harry," Mr. Prescott replied, "that you are trying to be more thoughtful of the feelings of others, and are resolved in future to conduct yourself in a manner befitting a true gentleman."

My story is already too long, and I have only to add that, when Harry had made his friend acquainted with the fate of their valentine, Fred was quite as much pleased as himself, and on his paying a visit to Mr. Prescott, and expressing his penitence and thanks in terms of sincerity which could not be doubted, that gentleman felt that both boys had received a valuable and lifelong lesson from Polly Hastings' valentine.

SECTION THREE

"How long will you torture me?
How long will you try to crush me with your words?
You have already insulted me ten times.
You should be ashamed of treating me so badly."
—Job 19:2, 3, NLT

It is safe to say that, in my entire lifetime, no story-poem has impacted my life as much as this one. It was never far from my father's side, and the only one he ever read aloud to me. It was also the favorite poem of Dr. James Dobson's mother. Down through the years, I have gone back to it again and again—chiefly because I too have had to fight a lifetime battle with my wayward tongue. In that respect, I maintain that no more powerful lines have ever been written than the poem's last six lines. And the most emotive single line is "My house had lost its soul; she was not there!" Not surprisingly, this true frontier poem became the signature work of Carleton's entire lifetime (1845–1912). It may seem a bit archaic language-wise at first, but stay with it—you'll always be glad you did! Most likely you'll agree with my wife's succinct review of it: "Very heart-wrenching."

THE FIRST SETTLER'S STORY

Will Carleton

It ain't the funniest thing a man can do—
Existing in a country when it's new;
Nature—who moved in first—a good
long while—
Has things already somewhat her own style,
And she don't want her woodland splendors
    battered,
Her rustic furniture broke up and scattered,
Her paintings, which long years ago were done
By that old splendid artist-king, the Sun,
Torn down and dragged in Civilization's gutter,
Or sold to purchase settlers' bread-and-butter.
She don't want things exposed, from porch to
    closet—
And so she kind o' nags the man who does it.
She carries in her pockets bags of seeds,
As general agent of the thriftiest weeds;
She sends her blackbirds, in the early morn,
To superintend his fields of planted corn;
She gives him rain past any duck's desire—
Then may be several weeks of quiet fire;
She sails mosquitoes—leeches perched on
    wings—

To poison him with blood-devouring stings;
She loves her ague-muscle to display,
And shake him up—say every other day;
With thoughtful, conscientious care, she makes
Those travellin' poison-bottles, rattlesnakes;
She finds time, 'mongst her other family cares,
To keep in stock good wild-cats, wolves, and
    bears;
She spurns his offered hand, with silent gibes,
And compromises with the Indian tribes
(For they who've wrestled with his bloody art
Say Nature always takes an Indian's part).
In short, her toil is every day increased,
To scare him out, and hustle him back East;
Till fin'lly, it appears to her someday,
That he has made arrangements for to stay;
Then she turns 'round, as sweet as anything,
And takes her new-made friend into the ring,
And changes from a snarl into a purr:
From mother-in-law to mother, as it were.

Well, when I first infested this retreat,
Things to my view looked frightful incomplete:

But Nature seemed quite cheerful, all about me.
A-carrying on her different trades without me.
These words the forest seemed at me to throw:
"Sit down and rest awhile before you go";
From bees to trees the whole woods seemed to
    say,
"You're welcome here till you can get away,
But not for time of any large amount;
So don't be hanging round on our account."
But I had come with heart-thrift in my song,
And brought my wife and plunder right along;
I hadn't a round-trip ticket to go back,
And if I had, there wasn't no railroad track;
And drivin' east was what I couldn't endure;
I hadn't started on a circular tour.

My girl-wife was as brave as she was good,
And helped me every blessed way she could;
She seemed to take to every rough old tree,
As sing'lar as when first she took to me.
She kep' our little log-house neat as wax;
And once I caught her fooling with my axe.
She learned a hundred masculine things to do:
She aimed a shot-gun pretty middlin' true,
Although, in spite of my express desire,
She always shut her eyes before she'd fire.
She hadn't the muscle (though she *had* the
    heart)
In outdoor work to take an active part;
Though in our firm of Duty & Endeavor,
She wasn't no silent partner whatsoever.
When I was logging, burning, choppin' wood—

She'd linger 'round, and help me all she could,
And kept me fresh-ambitious all the while,
And lifted tons, just with her voice and smile.
With no desire my glory for to rob,
She used to stan' around and boss the job;
And when first-class success my hands befell,
Would proudly say "*We* did that pretty well!"
She *was* delicious, both to hear and see—
That pretty wife-girl that kep' house for me!

Church days, we didn't propose, for lack o'
    church,
To have our souls left wholly in the lurch;
And so I shaved and dressed up, well's I could,
And did a day's work trying to be good.
My wife was always bandbox-sleek; and when
Our fat old bull's-eye watch said half past ten
('Twas always varying from the narrow way,
And lied on church days, same as any day),
The family Bible from its high perch started
(The one her mother gave her when they
    parted),
The hymn-book, full of music-balm and
    fire—
The one she used to sing in in the choir—
One I sang with her from—I've got it yet—
The very first time that we *really* met;
(I recollect, when first our voices gibed,
A feeling that declines to be described!
And when our eyes met—near the second
    verse—
A kind of old-acquaintance look in hers,

And something went from mine, which, I de-
clare,
I never even knew before was there—
And when our hands touched—slight as slight
could be—
A streak o' sweetened lightnin' thrilled through
me!
But that's enough of that; perhaps, even now,
You'll think I'm softer than the law'll allow;
But you'll protect an old man with his age,
For yesterday I turned my eightieth page;
Besides, there'd be less couples falling out
If such things were more freely talked about.)

Well, we would take these books, sit down
alone,
And have a two-horse meeting, all our own;
And read our verses, sing our sacred rhymes,
And make it seem a good deal like old times.
But finally across her face there'd glide
A sort of sorry shadow from inside;
And once she dropped her head, like a tired
flower,
Upon my arm, and cried a half an hour.
I humored her until she had it out,
And didn't ask her what it was about.
I knew right well: our reading, song, and
prayer
Had brought the old times back, too true and
square.
The large attended meetings morn and night;
The spiritual and mental warmth and light;

Her father, in his pew, next to the aisle;
Her mother, with the mother of her smile;
Her brothers' sly, forbidden church-day glee;
Her sisters, e'en a'most as sweet as she;
Her girl and boy friends, not too warm or
cool;
Her little scrub class in the church-day school;
The social, and the singings and the ball;
And happy home-cheer waiting for them
all—
These marched in close procession through
her mind,
And didn't forget to leave their tracks behind.
You married men—there's many in my
view—
Don't think your wife can all wrap up in you,
Don't deem though close her life to yours
may grow,
That you are all the folks she wants to know;
Or think your stitches form the only part
Of the crochet-work of a woman's heart.
Though married souls each other's lives may
burnish,
Each needs some help the other cannot fur-
nish.

Well, neighborhoods meant counties, in those
days;
The roads didn't have accommodating ways;
And maybe weeks would pass before she'd
see—
And much less talk with—any one but me.

The Indians sometimes showed their sun-
baked faces,
But they didn't teem with conversational
graces;
Some ideas from the birds and trees she stole,
But 'twasn't like talking with a human soul;
And finally I thought that I could trace
A half heart-hunger peering from her face.
Then she would drive it back, and shut the
door;
Of course that only made me see it more.
'Twas hard to see her give her life to mine,
Making a steady effort not to pine;
'Twas hard to hear that laugh bloom out each
minute,
And recognize the seeds of sorrow in it.
No misery makes a close observer mourn,
Like hopeless grief with hopeful courage
borne;
There's nothing sets the sympathies to paining.
Like a complaining woman, uncomplaining!
It always draws my breath out into sighs,
To see a brave look in a woman's eyes.

Well, she went on, as plucky as could be,
Fighting the foe she thought I did not see,
And using her heart-horticultural powers
To turn that forest to a bed of flowers.
You can not check an unadmitted sigh,
And so I had to soothe her on the sly,
And secretly to help her draw her load;
And soon it came to be an uphill road.

Hard work bears hard upon the average pulse,
Even with satisfactory results;
But when effects are scarce, the heavy strain
Falls dead and solid on the heart and brain.
And when we're bothered, it will oft occur
We seek blame-timber; and I lit on her;
And looked at her with daily lessening favor,
For what I knew she couldn't help, to save
her.
(We often—what our minds should blush
with shame for—
Blame people most for what they're least to
blame for.)
Then there'd be a misty, jealous thought oc-
cur,
Because I wasn't Earth and Heaven to her,
And all the planets that about us hovered,
And several more that hadn't been discovered;
And my hard muscle-labor, day by day,
Deprived good-nature of the right of way;
And 'tain't no use—this trying to conceal
From hearts that love us—what our own
hearts feel;
They can't escape close observation's mesh—
And thoughts have tongues that are not made
of flesh.
And so ere long she caught the half-grown
fact:
Commenced observing how I didn't act;
And silently began to grieve and doubt
O'er old attentions now sometimes left out—
Some kind caress—some little petting ways—

Commenced a-staying in on rainy days
(I did not see 't so clear then, I'll allow;
But I can trace it rather acc'rate now);
And Discord, when he once had called and
    seen us,
Came round quite often, and edged in be-
    tween us.

One night, I came from work unusual late,
Too hungry and too tired to feel first-rate—
Her supper struck me wrong (though I'll al-
    low
She hadn't much to strike with, anyhow);
And when I went to milk the cows, and found
They'd wandered from their usual feeding
    ground,
And maybe 'd left a few long miles behind 'em,
Which I must copy, if I mean to find 'em,
Flash-quick the stay-chains of my temper
    broke,
And in a trice these hot words I had spoke:
"You ought to 've kept the animals in view,
And drove 'em in; you'd nothing else to
    do.
The heft of all our life on me must fall;
You just lie round, and let me do it all."

That speech—it hadn't been gone a half a
    minute,
Before I saw the cold black poison in it;
And I'd have given all I had, and more,
To 've only safely got it back in-door.

I'm now what most folks "well-to-do" would
    call:
I feel today as if I'd give it all,
Provided I through fifty years might reach,
And kill and bury that half-minute speech. . . .

She handed back no words, as I could hear;
She didn't frown—she didn't shed a tear;
Half proud, half crushed, she stood and
    looked me o'er,
Like someone she had never seen before!
But such a sudden anguish-lit surprise
I never viewed before in human eyes.
(I've seen it oft enough since, in a dream;
It sometimes wakes me, like a midnight
    scream!)

That night, while theoretically sleeping,
I half heard and half felt that she was weeping;
And my heart then projected a design
To softly draw her face up close to mine,
And beg of her forgiveness to bestow,
For saying what we both knew wasn't so.
I've got enough of this world's goods to do
    me,
And make my nephews painfully civil to me:
I'd give it all to know she only knew
How near I came to what was square and true.
But somehow, every single time I'd try,
Pride would appear, and kind o' catch my eye
And hold me, on the edge of my advance,
With the cold steel of one sly, scornful glance.

Next morning, when, stone-faced, but heavy-
  hearted,
With dinner pail and sharpened axe I started
Away for my day's work—she watched the
  door,
And followed me halfway to it or more;
And I was just a-turning round at this,
And asking for my usual good-bye kiss;
But on her lip I saw a proudish curve,
And in her eye a shadow of reserve;
And she had shown—perhaps half unawares—
Some little independent breakfast airs—
And so the usual parting didn't occur,
Although her eyes invited me to her,
Or rather half invited me; for she
Didn't advertise to furnish kisses free:
You always had—that is, I had—to pay
Full market price, and go more 'n half the way.
So, with a short "Good-bye," I shut the door,
And left her as I never had before.

Now, when a man works with his muscle
  smartly,
It makes him up into machinery, partly;
And any trouble he may have on hand
Gets deadened like, and easier to stand.
And though the memory of last night's mistake
Bothered me with a dull and heavy ache,
I all the forenoon gave my strength full rein,
And made the wounded trees bear half the pain.
But when at noon my lunch I came to eat,
Put up by her so delicately neat—

Choicer, somewhat, than yesterday's had
  been,
And some fresh, sweet-eyed pansies she'd put
  in—
"Tender and pleasant thoughts," I knew they
  meant—
It seemed as if her kiss with me she'd sent;
Then I became once more her humble lover,
And said, "Tonight I'll ask forgiveness of her."

I went home over-early on that eve,
Having contrived to make myself believe,
By various signs I kind o' knew and guessed,
A thunderstorm was coming from the west.
('Tis strange, when one sly reason fills the
  heart,
How many honest ones will take its part;
A dozen first-class reasons said 'twas right
That I should strike home early on that night.)

Half out of breath, the cabin door I swung,
With tender heart-words trembling on my
  tongue;
But all within looked desolate and bare;
My house had lost its soul—she was not there!
A penciled note was on the table spread,
And these are something like the words it said:
"The cows have strayed again, I fear;
I watched them pretty close; don't scold me,
  dear.
And where they are, I think I *nearly* know:
I heard the bell not very long ago—

I've hunted for them all the afternoon;
I'll try once more—I think I'll find them soon.
Dear, if a burden I have been to you,
And haven't helped you as I ought to do,
Let old-time memories my forgiveness plead;
I've tried to do my best—I have, indeed.
Darling, piece out with love the strength I lack,
And have kind words for me when I get back."

Scarce did I give this letter sight and tongue—

Some swift-blown raindrops to the window clung,
And from the clouds a rough, deep growl proceeded;
My thunderstorm had come, now 'twasn't needed.
I rushed out-door; the air was stained with black;
Night had come early, on the storm cloud's back.
And every thing kept dimming to the sight,
Save when the clouds threw their electric light;
When, for a flash, so clean-cut was the view,
I'd think I saw her—knowing 'twas not true.
Through my small clearing dashed wide sheets of spray,
As if the ocean waves had lost their way;

Scarcely a pause the thunder-battle made,
In the bold clamor of its cannonade.
And she, while I was sheltered, dry and warm,
Was somewhere in the clutches of this storm!
She who, when storm-frights found her at her best,
Had always hid her white face on my breast!

My dog, who'd skirmished 'round me all the day,
Now, crouched and whimpering, in a corner lay;
I dragged him by the collar to the wall—
I pressed his quivering muzzle to a shawl—
"Track her, old boy!" I shouted: and he whined,
Matched eyes with me, as if to read my mind—
Then with a yell went tearing through the wood.
I followed him, as faithful as I could.
No pleasure-trip was that, through flood and flame!
We raced with death;—we hunted noble game.
All night we dragged the woods without avail;
The ground got drenched—we could not keep the trail.
Three times again my cabin home I found,
Half hoping she might be there, safe and sound;
But each time 'twas an unavailing care:

My house had lost its soul; she was not there!

When, climbing the wet trees, next morning-sun
Laughed at the ruin that the night had done,
Bleeding and drenched—by toil and sorrow
    bent—
Back to what used to be my home I went.
But, as I neared our little clearing-ground—
Listen!—I heard the cowbell's tinkling sound;
The cabin door was just a bit ajar;
It gleamed upon my glad eyes like a star!
"Brave heart," I said, "for such a fragile form!
She made them guide her homeward through
    the storm!"
Such pangs of joy I never felt before:
"You've come!" I shouted, and rushed through
    the door.

Yes, she had come—and gone again.—She lay
With all her young life crushed and wrenched
    away—
Lay—the heart-ruins of our home among—
Not far from where I killed her with my
    tongue.
The raindrops glittered 'mid her hair's long
    strands,

The forest-thorns had torn her feet and hands,
And 'midst the tears—brave tears—that one
    could trace
Upon the pale but sweetly resolute face,
I once again the mournful words could read—
"I've tried to do my best—I have, indeed."

And now I'm mostly done; my story's o'er;
Part of it never breathed the air before.
'Tisn't over-usual, it must be allowed,
To volunteer heart-history to a crowd,
And scatter 'mongst them confidential tears,
But you'll protect an old man with his years;
And wheresoe'er this story's voice can reach,
This is the sermon I would have it preach:

Boys flying kites haul in their white-winged
    birds;
You can't do that when you're flying words.
"Careful with fire," is good advice, we know:
"Careful with words," is ten times doubly so.
Thoughts unexpressed may sometimes fall back
    dead;
But God himself can't kill them once they're said!
    (Italics added)

*S*elf-control—so many athletes today lack it. Like petulant little children, they smash golf clubs or tennis racquets, they attack people on the opposing team, and they end up belittling themselves in front of millions. But, to a lesser extent, all through my life I've battled my temper. Said things I'm instantly sorry for. Written letters that almost burn the paper—fortunately, I tend to avoid mailing them until I cool down. Then I tear them up. This is just such a story.

The Girl Who Conquered Herself

Margaret Sangster

Ruth always had an ungovernable temper. I have known Ruth a long while—we played dolls together, and made mud pies and divided our candy, and so I really know. I am perhaps her very first friend. Of course her real name is not Ruth, but I am rather sure that it would be unfair to tell her real name.

My first memory of Ruth's temper is a bit dim, for we might have been five years old, we two, at the time. I remember that I owned a black-faced woolly-headed doll, and I remember that she wanted it for her own. Because I was not the giving-up kind—primarily, however, because I loved the doll—I refused to give it up, whereupon Ruth threw a stone at me. It was a large, sharp stone, and it made an ugly looking, jagged little cut on my forehead. I remember how the blood dripped down the side of my face.

Ruth was aghast at the mischief she had done. I can see her now, her chubby baby hands clasped in front of her eyes to shut out the sight of the blood. At my wails someone came to me and washed my face, and put sticking plaster on my forehead. I was kissed and petted and given a peppermint stick. But, most of all (and this memory is a very real one), I can see Ruth's small, stricken face, and I can hear her voice saying—

"I didn't mean to! I didn't mean to hurt her! The stone frew itself!"

My forehead was nearly well the next day. In a week the scar of it was quite gone. But it was a long time before the scared look was entirely driven from Ruth's eyes.

We went right on being friends. A hastily flung rock or a cut forehead is a small thing to a really true child-friendship. But, though we continued to be friends, we saw less and less of each other as the years went on. We were well past the doll and mud-pie stage, and were living in different towns and going to different schools and having different interests in life, and different friends. But occasionally we visited. It was on one of my visits to her home that I again saw her lose her temper. It was when her small brother spilled a cup of chocolate on her new dress. I'll admit that she had a provocation, for it was a wonderful dress; but her little brother hadn't meant to spill the chocolate.

Ruth was a pretty girl. She was still a pretty girl, for she has a great mass of corn-colored hair and the bluest eyes I ever saw. She had a mouth that looked like the first rosebud of June. But though Ruth is a pretty girl, I was glad I was not her little brother that day when he spilled the chocolate on her gown. Her blue eyes grew as hard and as cold as ice—as ice with some dark fire glowing behind it— and her rosebud mouth straightened out until it looked like a thin crimson gash on her face. I saw her hand clutch convulsively on the air, and then all at once the little brother gave a queer gasp and ran out of the room. I didn't blame him at all, for, strangely, at that moment I remembered an angry baby face and a wildly flung stone. And across the years that divided my little childhood from my big girlhood, the hurt of my cut forehead came back to me.

And then, in a moment, Ruth's clutched hand unfolded, and her lips parted in a cold smile that was almost a sneer. "The dress will wash," I ventured, half frightened.

"Yes," said Ruth. And then suddenly she picked up a cup—an empty chocolate cup of very fine china—and threw it down—hard—on the floor. I watched, dazedly, as it shattered into a hundred bits. And then Ruth burst into sobs, and ran from the room. Upstairs I could hear her bedroom door slam and the lock snap quickly.

I stood alone in the room, looking at the fragments of the cup, lying about on the floor, and as I stood there her little brother came strolling back.

"Did Ruth—throw that?" he questioned, pointing to the pieces. And then, before I could answer, he grinned, in an apologetic, small-boy way.

"Ruth's a dandy girl, usually," he told me. "She's an awful nice girl. But when anything makes her mad—whew! She's just awful. She screams an' cries, an' throws things. An' she doesn't care who she hits. She's always sorry— after—but she can't seem to help actin' like she does!"

Ruth was upstairs the rest of the day with a bad headache. The next day she was down early, singing as she dusted the rooms. But her face was pale, and her eyes were a bit scared.

We grew up even more, from the big-girl stage to young ladies with their hair up. We had left school. I was launched in the business world, doing the work I love to do, when Ruth announced her engagement. Her fiancé was a Western man, and she had not known him for a very long time. She had never met any of his relatives, but she wrote me that his father, who was a famous surgeon, was going to spend a week in the city, and that she was going to give a dinner for him.

"I'll be coming into town the day of the dinner," she wrote, "and if you'll meet me in the station we'll go up together. I want to get there before Bob's father comes. I want him to see me looking my best."

And I said I would come to the dinner and meet her wherever she wanted me to.

I went to the station, and though it was not long before train time, Ruth was nowhere to be seen. I waited nervously, for I remembered that she wanted to get home early—that she wanted "Bob's father to see her at her best." And then at last, just as the iron gates had slammed shut—just as the whistle of the train had tooted for the last time, Ruth dashed into the station, her face scarlet from running, her hat on one side.

"The train is ready to go," I told her; "they've shut us out."

The train station was full of people, but Ruth didn't care. She turned to the guard who had shut the gate: "Let me through," she beseeched him; "it's important that I get this train. I *must* get it."

But the guard stood firm. "Sorry, lady," he told her, "but it's against the rules."

And then Ruth lost her temper, as I had seen her lose it when she hit me with a stone

and when her brother had spilled the chocolate. The flush faded out of her face, leaving it pale and sharp and worn.

"I hate you!" she said to the guard. "I hate you! You might have let me through. I hate you!" Her foot stamped on the ground, and with all her might she threw a paper package across the station. It struck a courtly old gentleman, and, bursting, fell at his feet. Pink rose petals littered the floor.

We were the center of a grinning crowd. I shrank back against a post and watched as the old gentleman picked up the roses and carried them to her.

"Young lady," he said, "I don't know who you are or what you are, but I want to tell you one thing. You've got to control that temper of yours, for it's hurting no one but yourself. It didn't hurt me when the package hit me. It only disgusted me. But it really did hurt you. If you keep on letting go of yourself, you'll land in an insane asylum. I *know*. And no one will be sorry to have you go there. For people with a temper like yours are a menace to any community."

Ruth stood pale and aghast. No one had ever talked to her that way. And the crowd, ever shifting, drifted away from where she stood. And just as the old man was going to speak again a young man, handsome, broadshouldered, and athletic, came up from behind and gripped his shoulder.

"Why, Dad," cried the young man, gladly, "how did you happen to find Ruth?"

And though I had never met him, I knew that it was Bob.

Late that night, after the guests had all retired, I went into Ruth's room. She was lying on her bed, sobbing, but she sat up at the sound of my step.

"I will never," she told me distinctly, "lose my temper again. And I will tell Bob everything tomorrow. Perhaps"—her voice broke—"perhaps he won't want to marry a girl who might end up in an insane asylum. But, no matter what happens, I will never lose my temper again."

And she never did. For Ruth made good—just as other girls make good with difficult problems. She told me that it was hard, desperately hard, at times. Sometimes she'd have to go up to her room and lock her door and bite her bedpost. Sometimes she would fall on her knees and ask God for help. But, no matter how much she wanted to give way—and I've seen her in some exasperating situations—she'd turn her back and hum a tune before she spoke. She told me that while she was humming she'd say "insane asylum" and "menace" over and over in her mind. And finally she won out, *for by controlling her temper she found that she had fewer occasions to lose it.*

I was visiting Ruth the other day in her new home. Her father-in-law, who loves her very much, lives with them. She does her own work, and after supper I went out into the kitchen and helped her wash the dishes. Bob dried them, and, manlike, he got interested in the conversation as he was drying Ruth's handsomest cut-glass, silver-mounted pitcher, and dropped it. It was one of her wedding presents, and I stepped back in very real fear before the expected storm. But the storm did not break.

"I'm sorry, dear," said Bob, humbly. "I'm awfully sorry." But Ruth cut him short.

"Don't you worry," she told him, soothingly. "We may get another someday, dear."

*M*y dearly beloved mother apparently never met a stranger in her life. In my case, it was not until I experienced one of my life's primary epiphanies after the untimely death of my own mentor, Dr. Walter Utt, chair of history at Pacific Union College, that I vowed, in gratitude to him, that I would, from that time on, make mentoring the number-one priority of my life. The results have been nothing short of astounding as God took my vow so seriously that every day He brings people into my life who either need what I can give them or give to me what I need.

This is just such a life-changing "unfinished" story, begun back in 1927. Most of my interactions, just as was true of Christ's heart-to-heart talk with the woman at the well, are cameos (only in the kingdom will I learn the rest of each story); all I do is seek to reach out, make a difference, in each interaction—and leave the rest to God.

A Chance Encounter

May Oakley

"VOLCANO IN FULL ERUPTION!" exclaimed Katherine Howell, as she unfolded the morning paper of July 8. "All Honolulu will be excited now." And she read aloud:

"Fire Pit Filling Up With Streams of Lava Gushing in From Great Fountains

"VOLCANO HOUSE, HAWAII, July 7, 9:45 P.M.—Madame Pele, mysteriously absent for three years, tonight is celebrating her homecoming with one of the most magnificent displays ever witnessed in the Halemaumau pit of Kilauea Volcano.

"Thousands of persons, from all parts of this island, are at the pit, enthralled by the big volcanic show, a dazzling demonstration.

"Three flaming fountains—one of the first four having united with the others—are pouring out a tremendous volume of lava.

"The eruption, which began with slight previous warning shortly after midnight this morning, has continued ceaselessly."

Katherine laid aside the paper with a weary gesture. "I suppose that I'll have to go racing over to Hawaii to see old Halemaumau spout. I've been there every time Madame Pele has sought to show off, and I must keep up my record."

The jingle of the telephone at her elbow interrupted her thoughts. She listened silently, then answered, "Yes, I've just read it. Well, I've seen every large eruption since I can remember—I'm quite an authority on Hawaiian volcanoes," she laughed. "I'm getting enthusiastic"—a long silence while she listened to the plan proposed over the telephone. "Really! I believe I'll go with you. The little steamer *Haleakala* will be crowded, so have

Richard buy our tickets early, Mina. I'll meet you at the pier at a quarter of four. Good-bye."

Katherine examined her list of social obligations, and as she telephoned several "regrets," she found that many of her friends were preparing for the same trip. The hurrying crowd at the pier was a surprise. As she stepped from the car and directed the chauffeur to return home, her waiting friends spied her.

"Doesn't look as if we are going," announced Mr. Burke, abruptly.

"Why not?"

"The ship was sold out to capacity before I got down here, and people are offering large sums for berths. Some are reselling their tickets. Aren't they excited? Mina." he addressed his wife. "If you girls were good sports, we could go over steerage. They are still selling steerage tickets. I really *want* to go. We may never have another chance—and we ought to see it. Think of living in Hawaii and never viewing that phenomenon of nature!" he waxed eloquent. "Come on, let's take a chance."

"Where will we sleep, Richard?"

"It is likely that we won't sleep. We'll perhaps be 'crowded in the cabin.' But it is only for one night. Say the word, and let's go. The time to see a volcano is when it is spouting."

Mrs. Burke yielded with a laugh. "I'll go if Katherine will."

"Get the tickets, Richard, and we'll try our luck," urged Katherine.

This was easier said than done, however, as whistles blew, baggage was hurried aboard, and sturdy Hawaiian workmen began to unloosen the ropes holding the gangplank.

"Please!" burst out Katherine, "we want to go aboard."

"Why don't you? Not a moment to lose, Miss."

"My husband hasn't come," began Mrs. Burke, when a firm hand propelled her up the gangplank, which the harbor men good naturedly held in place. A swift backward glance disclosed her husband struggling with the baggage and Katherine close behind him.

Bang! went the gangplank, and with a last warning toot the little steamer began to move.

"We're off, girls!" shouted Mr. Burke. "That was a close shave."

The *Haleakala* lost no time in getting out to sea with her heavy burden of sightseers. Past the famous beach of Waikiki, the forts, the magnificent hotels, historic old Diamond Head with its outstanding lighthouse, beaches fringed with palms, and then the island of Oahu faded into the distance. A strong wind and heavy seas tossed the little steamer to and fro.

The passengers who were accustomed to traveling steerage began to make themselves as comfortable as possible. Some opened their various bundles and spread pallets whereupon they deposited the sleeping children; others grouped around a young boy twangling a ukulele, and sang lustily; many were eating. The lunches were surprisingly characteristic of the nationalities represented.

Mrs. Burke looked with positive disgust upon the scene. "If one was obsessed with the mania for helping the downtrodden masses, he wouldn't have far to go," she whispered.

"Let's get out on the deck," her husband suggested, "if this pitching continues—I—well—I prefer to be outside."

"Richard! Haven't I heard you boast of being a good sailor?" bantered Katherine.

"I don't call this sailing," he replied, weakly.

"You'd feel better if you had food. We didn't prepare for this emergency as the wise ones in there did," she said, indicating the steerage cabin.

A tall girl standing by the rail turned to her eagerly. "Pardon me, but I have food. Won't you let me share it with you?" Her sincere manner impressed Katherine.

"If we won't rob you. I'm famished," she agreed, frankly.

"It won't rob me."

Encouraged by the friendly attitude of the three young people, the girl continued. "You see, I didn't know what to expect when I reached Hilo, so I'm prepared." She unfastened a suitcase at her feet and drew out several packages.

"Here is a box of sandwiches and here are some hard-boiled eggs and fruit," the girl said.

"There is plenty," agreed Katherine. "We'll help you with this, and then get you more when we reach Hilo in the morning. We are on our way to the volcano, and didn't know we were coming steerage, where no meals are provided."

"I also am going to see the volcano, but you see by this that I knew *I* was going steerage. There is no place to sit, is there?" questioned the stranger. "I've had the most interesting time watching the Japanese mothers put their babies to bed in every available space. I have a blanket here. Let me spread it out, and we can sit down close to the rail. We'll get fresh air, at least."

"That isn't all we're getting," grumbled Mrs. Burke, as a huge wave struck the ship and sent a shower of spray over them.

"You'll get worse than spray before you view Halemaumau!" retorted Katherine, who believed in playing the game, now that they had started.

"Well, I can't stand this." Mrs. Burke shook her skirts in disdain and moved away.

"I'll take a sandwich, if I may, and follow her," groaned Mr. Burke.

"This is an adventure for me. My name is Lorene Crane," began the girl. "It didn't take me long to decide that I must see that volcano."

"Are you *kamaaina*?" questioned Katherine.

"I've heard that word before, but I don't know whether I'm it or not," laughed Miss Crane.

"That means an old resident."

"Then I'm not, but I've been here long enough to discover that there is rejoicing in these islands when a volcano begins to rumble and explode and send up fountains of red-hot lava."

"The old Hawaiians say," explained Katherine, "that the volcano is the home of a goddess, Pele, and when it is quiet, they believe she leaves her home because she is angry. They throw all sorts of offerings into the fire pit to appease her wrath. When the volcano begins to boil and sputter, they say Madame Pele has returned and is stirring her pot. Weren't you afraid of the reports of our volcano?"

"Somewhat, before I came over. I couldn't imagine what a real live volcano was like— and I can't yet, for that matter."

Katherine sank down upon the blanket. "I'll stay with you out here. I don't mind getting sprayed. It's worse in there, crying babies, and seasick folks everywhere." She smiled at her young companion.

"Tell me how you come to be going over alone?"

The girl hastily turned her face toward the open sea.

Katherine was visibly embarrassed by the silence that followed. "Pardon me," she whispered, "that was a rude question."

The girl met her apology with a square look. "No, I'll tell you. I travel alone, because I *am* all alone."

"I'm sorry," murmured Katherine.

"My mother had been sick for a long time, and the doctors advised a change. At last we decided to come here. We didn't see how we *could* do it, but we did. She seemed to improve until last month, and now she is gone."

"Oh!" exclaimed Katharine. "Why did I ask that question?"

"I'm glad that you took enough interest in me to ask. It is good to have someone to talk with."

Katherine reached for her hand in the darkness. "Do tell me," she urged.

"Mother and I had always been together, and we always talked over everything. You can't imagine what an emptiness there is now. I was taking the nurses' course. I had to drop out when we came over here. It was necessary for me to make our living, and I couldn't leave Mother to nurse, so I got a place to work as stenographer. My employer is having a hard struggle; and this morning when I went to the office, he met me with the announcement that he would not need me for a week, and perhaps not any more at all. On the way back to my boarding house, I heard the great news about the volcano, and reasoned with myself, or at least I persuaded myself, that I might be able to go. Here I was, idle for a week. I ran down to the steamship company, and found I could go cheaply if I was willing to ride back here, so I decided to venture. Do you think it was terrible foolish?"

"Not at all!" Katherine reassured her. "How fortunate that we met you. I have been there before, so I'll tell about what I have seen, and you will be somewhat prepared for the wonderful awe-inspiring sight that will meet our eyes tomorrow."

The early morning light found the two girls still snuggled up on the blanket.

"You're coming with us, Lorene," decided Katherine, as they disembarked at Hilo.

"I'd love to," Lorene answered her newfound friend, "but you know I have to consider expense. Doubtless you and your friends—"

"But you are my friend." Katherine had a way of settling things. "Mr. Burke has ordered a car to meet us. There are thousands of people flocking to the Kilauea district."

Lorene felt herself hurried through the throng and into the car. Thrilling! She listened in wonder to Katherine's terse sentences of explanation. "Those are tree ferns. Around this curve you'll get a marvelous view. We'll soon reach the Volcano House. Some say it is located over a seething field of lava."

Great caravans of automobiles, and many people on foot, were wending their way to the pit. The tremendous bowl, like a spacious cavern, was filling with red-hot, white-hot lava. Huge fountains of lava played here and there. Lorene, following the example of the braver sightseers, lay flat on the brink and gazed far, far below into the depths. Time and all else were forgotten. She was fascinated with the grandeur of the awful sight before her. As a geyser of lava blew up to three hundred feet in height, the onlookers crept back from the edge. Exclamations of "Marvelous!" "Wonderful!" "Thrilling!" and even "Frightful!" were heard. Lorene watched a giant cone about sixty feet in height being formed around a fountain of boiling lava that was shooting at least one hundred feet higher, creating a river that flowed into the fire lake in the bottom of the pit.

Mr. Burke roused her. "They say this ledge is unsafe, Miss Crane. There is a huge crack between you and solid earth. If it should break off, it's a long way down there." He pointed into the crater.

"Is there solid earth anywhere?" questioned Lorene. "I feel doubts after looking into that exploding pit."

Two days they spent watching the volcano in all its changing moods, and then, after a hurried trip over the rest of the island, took their departure.

"This wharf looks good to me," groaned Mr. Burke when they were safely ashore in Honolulu, "even if it does seem to be twisting and rolling and pitching and jerking."

"I'm glad that I went," put in Katherine, loyally.

"I'm happy," declared Lorene, and her tired eyes sparkled.

"We'll soon forget the experiences of the passage and remember only the glories of the volcano, eh, Mina?"

"All I can think of now is home and bed, but I'm glad that we went."

The Howell car stood waiting. Katherine slipped her arm through Lorene's.

"Come home with me, won't you?"

"Thank you. I must not. You have been wonderful to me, and I can never thank—"

"Lorene," interrupted Katherine, as she drew her toward the car, "we cemented a friendship when you shared your blanket with me, that I want to be lifelong. You can be a real help. Jump in and let me tell you about it. The night we became acquainted," she went on to say as the car rolled along, "something came to life in my heart that I can't explain. It has been bumping and thumping away for expression ever since. You inspired me, Lorene, with a burning desire to be of some real use in the world."

"You! With your education, your personality, and—I begin to suspect—your wealth."

"Still, my dear, as you told me of your life with your mother, and your struggle for an education, and your enthusiasm over your work in the hospital, your anxiety to get back to it, I felt humble and useless. Then and there, crouched on your blanket and hanging to the rail, I made a resolution that I would spend the rest of my life in helping others."

"You do." Lorene defended her. "Just see what you have done for me. You gave me the most wonderful vacation."

"I did it, yes—selfishly. I wanted to be near you."

On the broad lanai of a beautiful home overlooking the sea, plans were made and unmade that night. Katherine's businesslike father, her society mother, and her invalid aunt joined the council.

Mr. Howell was speedily won over to his daughter's point of view. Her frivolous mother still voiced grim forebodings that Katherine would be disgusted with sick folks and ready to return after a week of the nurse's training.

"At least, Mother, give me my week."

"What if you should get smallpox and ruin your complexion?"

"What if I should, Mother, others have. Aunt Alice, if I am of any help to anyone in this household it is to you, and you'll spare me? My heart is in this thing."

The invalid answered, impulsively, "I'll

spare you, Katherine, though I'll miss you sorely."

Stories are supposed to have pleasant endings, but this one hasn't ended yet, so we can only leave you with a memory of two girls sailing for the mainland—one to take up her cherished work where she left it, and the other filled with a determination to train for service.

*N*ever can I forget that day: a dear friend and I were both competing for the same executive position, and we were both equally qualified for it. Turned out he got the position instead of me. Rather than congratulate him, I telephoned him, informing him that he'd been given the position, but that people everywhere were saying it was undeserved. It was the most poisonous telephone call I ever made. Though I later abjectly apologized to him, the damage to our friendship was done and could not be undone.

Like the Ruth in this story, I have had to live with it for almost half a century now. No small thanks to my despicable call, it caused me to prayerfully rethink my lust for administrative supremacy. In time, I finally gained the victory, recognizing that nothing is more ephemeral than one's place in an administrative pecking order.

WHAT ONE LIE DID

Author Unknown

It was winter twilight. Shadows moved about the room with noiseless feet, while the ruddy light flickered pleasantly between the ancient andirons. A venerable old lady, whose hair old time had silvered, but whose heart he had left fresh and young, sat musing in an armchair, drawn up closely by the fireside. Suddenly the door opened, and fairy footsteps bounded to her side.

"Well, Bessie," said the old lady, laying her hand lovingly on the child's sunny ringlets, "have you had a good slide?"

"Beautiful, Aunt Ruth; and now won't you tell me one of your nice stories?"

Bessie was an only child. Her mother had recently died, and Bessie had come to visit her aunt, of whose heart she at once took possession by her winning ways and affectionate disposition. But Aunt Ruth's eyes were of the clear sort, and she soon discovered that Bessie was not only unscrupulous as to the truth, but that she displayed little sensitiveness when detected in a falsehood. Now, if there was any one trait for which Aunt Ruth was particularly distinguished, it was her unswerving rectitude; if there was any one thing that annoyed her more than all others, it was anything that came under the heading of falsehood. It was the language of her heart, "A liar shall not stand in my sight" (Psalm 101:7). She determined, with the help of God, to root out from her darling's character the noxious weed, whatever effort it might cost her. Of this she had been musing, and her resolve was formed.

"Get your cricket, dear, and come close beside me;" and in a moment the child's blue eyes were upturned to hers.

"I am old now, Bessie," and she tenderly stroked that fair brow, "and my memory is failing. But I can recall the time when I was a little dancing, sunny-haired girl, like you. You open your eyes wonderingly, but, if your life is spared, before you know it, child, you will be an old lady like Aunt Ruth.

"In those young days I was in a spelling class, at school, with a little girl named Amy, a sweet-tempered, sensitive child, and a very good scholar. She seemed disposed to cling to me, and I could not very well resist her timid advances. Yet I did not quite like her, because she often went above me in the class, when, but for her, I should have stood at the head. Poor Amy could not account for my occasional coolness, for I was too proud to let her know the reason. I had been a truthful child, Bessie, but envy tempted me, and I yielded. I sometimes tried to prejudice the other girls against Amy, and this was the beginning of my deceit. She was too shy to defend herself, and so I usually carried my point.

"One day our teacher gave out to us the word, *believe.* In her usual low voice Amy spelled 'b-e-l-i-e-v-e, believe.'

"Our teacher misunderstanding her said, quickly, 'Wrong—the next,' but turning to her again, asked, 'Did you not spell it l-e-i-v-e?'

" 'No, ma'am, I said l-i-e-v-e.' Miss R——, still in doubt, looking at me, inquired, 'You heard Ruth; how was it?' A wicked thought occurred to me—to disgrace her, and raise myself.

"Deliberately I uttered a gross falsehood, 'Amy said l-e-i-v-e.' The teacher turned toward her, and, confounded by my accusation, she was silent, while her flushed face and streaming eyes gave her the appearance of guilt. 'Amy,' said her teacher sternly, 'I did not expect a lie from you. Go, now, to the foot of the

class, and remember to remain after school.'

"I had triumphed, Bessie; Amy was disgraced, and I stood proudly at the head of my class, but I was not happy.

"When school was dismissed, I pretended to have lost something, and lingered in the hall. I heard the teacher say, 'Amy, come here,' and then I caught the light footsteps of the gentle child.

" 'How could you tell that lie?'

" 'Miss R——, I did not tell a lie,' but even as she denied it, I could see through the keyhole that in her grief at the charge, and her dread of punishment, she stood trembling like a culprit.

" 'Hold out your hand.'

"There I stood, as if spellbound. Stroke after stroke of the hard ruler I heard fall upon the small white hand of the innocent child. You may well hide your eyes from me, Bessie. Oh, why did I not speak? Every stroke went to my heart, but I would not confess my sin, and so I stole softly from the door. As I lingered on the way, Amy walked slowly along, with her books in one hand, while with the other she kept wiping away the tears, which yet would not cease to flow. Her sobs seeming to come from a breaking heart sank deep into my own. As she walked weepingly on, her foot stumbled, she fell, and her books were scattered on the ground. I picked them up and handed them to her. Turning toward me her soft blue eyes, swimming in tears, in the sweetest tones, she said,—

" 'I thank you, Ruth.'

"It made my guilty heart beat faster, but I would not speak; so we went on silently together.

"When I reached home, I said to myself, 'What is the use? Nobody knows it, and why should I be so miserable?' I resolved to throw off the hated burden, and, going into the pleasant parlor, I talked and laughed as if nothing were the matter. But the load on my poor heart only grew the heavier. I needed no one, Bessie, to tell me the wages of sin. The eye of God seemed consuming me. But the worse I felt, the gayer I seemed; and more than once I was scolded for my boisterous mirth, while tears were struggling to escape.

"At length I went to my room. I could not pray, and so hurrying to bed, I resolutely shut my eyes. But sleep would not come to me. The ticking of the old clock in the hall seemed every moment to grow louder, as if reproaching me; and when it slowly tolled the hour of midnight, it smote upon my ear like a knell. I turned and turned upon my little pillow, but it was filled with thorns. Those sweet blue eyes, swimming in tears, were ever before me; the repeated strokes of the hard ruler kept sounding in my ears. At length, unable to endure it longer, I left my bed, and sat down by the window. The noble elms stood peacefully in the moonlight, the penciled shadow of their spreading branches lying tremulously on the ground. The white fence, the graveled walks, the perfect quietness in which everything without was wrapped, seemed to mock my restlessness, while the solemn midnight sky filled me with awe I never felt before. Ah! Bessie, a reproving conscience and an angry God are too hard for a child to wrestle with!

"As I turned from the window, my eyes rested on the snow-white coverlet of my little bed, a birthday gift from my mother. All her patient kindness swept into my mind. I felt her dying hand upon my head. I listened once more to her fluttering voice, as she fervently besought the blessing of heaven upon her first-born. 'Oh, make her a truthful, holy child!' I tried to banish from my thoughts this last petition of my dying mother; but the more resolute was my purpose, the more distinctly did those pleading tones fall upon my heart, till bowing upon the window, I wept convulsively. But tears, Bessie, could give me no relief.

"My agony became every moment more intense, till at length, I rushed, almost in terror, to my father's bedside.

" 'Father! Father!' But I could say no more. Tenderly putting his arms around me, he laid my throbbing head upon his chest; and there he gently soothed me, till I could so far control the torrent, as to explain its cause. Then, how fervently did he plead with heaven, that his sinning child might be forgiven!

" 'Dear Father,' said I, 'will you go with me tonight to see poor Amy?'

"He answered, 'Tomorrow morning, my child.'

"Delay was torture; but, striving to suppress my disappointment, I received my father's kiss and went back to my room. But slumber still fled from my weary eyelids. My longing to beg Amy's forgiveness amounted to a frenzy; and after watching for the morning, for what seemed to me hours, my anguish became so intolerable that I fled once more to my father, and with tears streaming down my cheeks, I knelt by his side, beseeching him to go with me to Amy that moment; adding, in a whisper, 'She may die before she has forgiven me.' He laid his hand upon my burning cheek and, after a moment's thought, replied,

" 'I will go with you, my child.'

"In a few moments we were on our way. As we approached Mrs. Sinclair's cottage, we perceived lights hurrying from one room to another. Shuddering with an undefinable dread, I drew closer to my father. He softly opened the gate and silently we passed through it.

"The doctor, who was just leaving the door, seemed greatly surprised to meet us there at that hour. Words cannot describe my feeling when in answer to my father's inquiries, he told us that Amy was sick with a brain fever.

" 'Her mother tells me,' he continued, 'that she has not been well for several days, but that she was unwilling to miss school. She came home yesterday afternoon, it seems, very unlike herself. She took no supper, but sat at the table mute, as if stupefied with grief. Her mother tried every way to draw from her the cause of her sorrow; but in vain. She went to bed with the same heartbroken appearance, and in less than an hour I was summoned. In her delirium she had been calling upon you, dear Ruth, beseeching you with the most mournful earnestness to pity and to save her.'

"Bessie, may you never know how his words pierced my heart!

"My earnest pleas to see Amy just one minute, prevailed with her widowed mother. Kindly taking my hand—murderer's—she led me to the sick chamber. As I looked on the sweet sufferer, all hope deserted me. The shadows of death were already on her forehead, and in her large blues eyes. Kneeling by her bed, in whispered words my heart pleaded, oh, so earnestly for forgiveness! But, when I looked entreatingly toward her, in her delirious gaze there was no recognition. No, Bessie! I never was to be comforted by the assurance of her pardon.

"When I next saw Amy, she was asleep. The bright flush had faded from her cheek, whose marble paleness was shaded by her long eyelashes. Delirium had ceased, and her aching heart was still. That small, white hand, which had been held out tremblingly, to receive the blows of the harsh ruler, now lay lovingly folded within the other. Never again would tears flow from those gentle eyes, nor that bosom heave with sorrow. That sleep was the sleep of death.

"My grief was wilder, if not deeper, than that mother's of whose lost treasure I had robbed her. She forgave me; but I could not forgive myself. What a long, long winter followed. My sufferings drove me into a fever, and in my delirium I called continually upon Amy. But God listened to the prayers of my dear father, and raised me from this sickness. And when the light footsteps of spring were seen upon the green earth, and early flowers were springing up around the grave of Amy, for the first time, I was allowed to visit it.

"My head swam, as I read, lettered so carefully on the white tablet:

AMY SINCLAIR
Fell asleep September third.

"Beside that fresh turf I knelt down, and offered, as I trust, the prayer of faith. I was there relieved, and strengthened too, Bessie," said Aunt Ruth, as she laid her hand tenderly upon that young head bowed down upon her lap. Poor Bessie's tears had long been flowing, and now her grief seemed uncontrollable. Nor did her aunt attempt consolation; for she hoped there was a healing in that sorrow.

"Pray for me!" whispered Bessie, as, at length, looking up through her tears, she flung her arms about her aunt; and from a full heart Aunt Ruth poured out her petitions in behalf of the weeping child.

That scene was never forgotten by Bessie; for in that dim hour, from the depths of her repentant tears, a light dawned upon her, brighter than the morning. And, although it had cost Aunt Ruth not a little to call up this shadow from the past, yet she felt repaid a thousandfold for her sacrifice. For that sweet young face, lovely as a May morning, but whose beauty had been often marred by workings of deceit and falsehood, grew radiant in the clear light of that truthful purpose which was then born in her soul.

*D*uring the years we lived in Texas, Harley Larkin lived in a home adjacent to ours. One time, he noticed the trouble I was having putting up a tree house for our son Greg and asked if we needed help. I said I did, meanwhile wondering how a one-armed man was going to be much help. In no time at all, he'd climbed the tall tree and—piece of cake—the tree house became a reality.

Needless to say, Harley Larkin was—and remains—a source of inspiration to everyone who knows him.

"He's Going to Die Anyway"

Harley Larkin

Though I knew logging was one of the most dangerous of all professions, never did I think I'd be one of its casualties. But since Dad was a logger, my brothers and I logged with him; logged with double-bit axes, crosscut saws, horses—and later on, chain saws.

After growing up, I married Charlotte, the love of my life, and we put down roots in Medford, Oregon. There, to keep food on the table for our family of four, I ran a successful commercial custodial service at night, and I worked with millowner B. F. Blank during the day, running the Hyster® forklift, head-saw, and trim saws.

One day, Jeff, a friend of mine, came by the mill yard, with a request: "My brother-in-law needs open-heart surgery. In order to pay for it, we plan to log his family's forty acres of timberland." Turns out I would be the one who ended up doing most of the logging.

But the day I shall never ever forget began just like any other. In the early dawn, as I walked across the landing, swirls of pumice dust engulfed my legs. We'd dragged so many logs across the rocky area that the resulting pumice powder was close to a foot deep, resembling nothing so much as a lunar landscape. I was unusually happy that morning, for only two more loads separated me from full-time work at White's Electronics (the world's then largest manufacturers of metal detectors). Things could hardly have been better.

Just two more loads.

I can see the setup now as clearly as though it happened just yesterday: Jeff had a bad habit of forgetting to put things back where they belonged. A few days before, instead of returning a discarded cast-iron shackle to its owner, he'd left it on a stump near the landing. Jeff, a respiratory therapist, was clueless as a logger; however, he was helping out that morning. Also helping out was a young man barely old enough to drive his father's truck. While the cat skinner and I were loading the last turn of logs, the young truck driver unwisely switched out the tongs for end-hooks, using the discarded cast-iron shackle in place of the steel one.

During the loading, I stood on the battery box behind the cab on the passenger side, next to the M-shaped steel headache rack, holding the rope tied to one end-hook so as to control log placement.

We then hoisted a twenty-two-inch diameter, thirty-two-foot-long sugar pine log above the truck, the heavy butt positioned in the saddle between two logs, with the lighter end hanging over the driver. As I leaned down to instruct the driver to move forward, the cast-iron shackle broke—in the process, launching the log straight at me. The log scoured my neck as it yanked me out of the truck and slammed me into the ground in front of the truck.

Whiteout ensued, and pumice filled my lungs. It seemed like the weight of the entire world was pressing down upon my chest. Try as I did, I could not even take a breath. It was like staying down too long, while swimming, and thinking *I'll never reach the surface in time*. As the dust cleared, help came. *Finally*, I was able to breathe again. When I asked for someone to lift my head so I could breathe easier, so sure were they that my neck was broken, that no one complied. Finally, I used my left hand to lift my head high enough to rest on a tin hat.

Then it hit! If I were to pour all the accumulated pain of a lifetime into one brief moment, it still could not have matched the excruciating pain induced by ripped nerves that now assailed me. *Everything* seemed magnified: sound, pain, and smell.

Charlotte was called and tersely informed that I had internal bleeding that appeared unstoppable; consequently, she was to inform the hospital to be ready for the ambulance bringing me in.

What followed is still a blur to me: just an unconnected series of disjointed images: hurried placement on a gurney, the rough ride on logging roads to the highway, an attendant bandaging my superficial wounds, then lying on a table in an emergency room foggily listening as three doctors discussed my condition. One of them instructed the nurses to not waste hospital time on me, concluding with these cruel words: "He's going to die anyway, so *let the undertaker clean him up*."

After another doctor said, "At any rate, he'd not ever be able to use *that* arm again," my mind segued to a one-armed high school student who used to wrestle with my roommate—the stench from that accident was so awful, we had to leave the window open for hours before we could stand to come back into our room. Those indelible images in my mind caused me to determine that, rather than face life without all my body parts, I'd just as soon not live at all.

That determination was not helped by the discovery that not only was the right scapula shattered, but *all the ribs on my right side were broken*. And that was but the beginning of their findings.

The pain was so terrible they were forced to pump a seemingly never-ending stream of morphine into my body. The result was that I lost all awareness of reality: visitors would come and go, but I was only foggily aware of them—and afterwards I could never remember that they'd been in my room at all.

I repeatedly tried to get the fingers of my paralyzed right arm to move—but to no avail. Each time I raised my head, motion sickness bordering on vomiting would invariably follow. But I never gave up: day or night, I kept trying.

Every two and a half minutes—it never varied—body-convulsing pain wracked my body. It felt like a broadsword was twirling and slashing inside me; it was accompanied by a sensation akin to having chicken wire relentlessly being dragged under the skin of my right arm. For the preservation of what sanity I had left, nurses were forced to administer liquid morphine every three hours. In this resulting drug-induced state, my mind played weird games. I kept saying things like, "Just give me an axe and I'll chop this club off."

Meanwhile, Charlotte spent hours at my bedside orally rehearsing the accident, as did doctors and nurses—but to no avail. I had no more memory than a dementia patient. At this juncture, providentially, Aura Maud, a nurse and former schoolmate of mine, told me that unless I switched to morphine pills, I would *never* recover. Miraculously, I remembered her counsel when the morning nurse came in to administer the usual shot, and thus requested the change.

A few hours later, I opened my eyes and was surprised to see Charlotte at my bedside. When I asked why she was there and what was happening, tired of answering the same questions, she sighed and said, "I'm not going to tell you again—you never remember anyway."

Her words really jolted me. Now I asked if she'd bring in our four-year-old daughter Kathy and two-year-old son Eugene. Most of all, I just wanted to go home! But how could that be possible when I couldn't even sit upright without nausea? Nurses threatened to tie me to the bed whenever I attempted to get out of it. Bed up, nausea . . . bed down . . . , up, nausea . . . , down, until finally equilibrium returned.

The next giant step was to swing my legs over the side of the bed; invariably, each time, I'd collapse, exhausted. The turning point proved to be a young, new nurse who gave me a bathrobe and slippers and helped me to stand. This was the first time since the accident that I had stood up. Then, miracle of miracles, the man who undertakers would clean up, took two unassisted steps!

By this time, the nurse, discovering I wasn't supposed to be out bed, lectured me and made threats if I got up again. But providentially, another nurse, unaware of my medical history, helped me to put on my bathrobe, slippers, and a waist belt. She then helped me walk out the door—but then she was forced to hang on to me for dear life as I rushed down the hall like something from a Munster movie. At that moment, it came to me that walking is nothing more than a regulated free fall. The nurse vainly kept telling me to slow down—but I couldn't until I reached the end of the hall and collapsed on an air-conditioning unit.

After ten days, the hospital sent me home with my paralyzed right arm in a sling. Charlotte now had the unenviable job of rolling, wiping, and feeding me. But now, with every sense exaggerated, I couldn't handle the noise my children made, so close friends made a temporary home for Kathy.

The never-ebbing pain resulted in sleep deprivation and exhaustion. The only thing that helped were capsules my doctor called "bombs." Within five minutes after taking one, I'd be asleep for ten-plus hours. Dependency and addiction were immediate.

It was then that Nonie (Charlotte's sister) quit her job and moved to Medford, Oregon, to take care of me. She walked me, pushing me far beyond what I deemed possible, threatening to leave me by the side of the road if I failed to keep going.

Not surprisingly, by this time our finances were so bad we were close to losing our home. Charlotte and I prayed continuously that somehow God would help us. And God spoke to Garey and Jenny—dear friends of ours. They had been laying aside every spare dollar in order to have enough money to buy a small home.

One day, as I lay alone on my bed praying, there was a knock on our door. Soon Garey and Jenny appeared at my bedside with a strange request: "Where is your house payment book?"

I answered, "Why do you need to know?"

"Because we're going to make your house payments," responded Jenny.

When I protested, Jenny asked, "Haven't you been praying that God would help you? Are you going to tell God no?"

What could I say? Garey and Jenny left with the payment book and made our house payments for six months.

Meanwhile, I had other problems: One was I couldn't even hold a cup with my left wrist. Turns out the center of the navicular bone was fractured. Monthly X-rays followed the casting of the bone. After six months, it was determined by the doctors that they'd remove bone chip from my hip and pack it in to fuse the navicular bone.

Before leaving the house for the final X-ray, I knelt by the side of my bed and prayed, "God, I have been through so much. If it would glorify Your name, I know You could heal me. Whatever Your will is OK with me. Thank You for whatever You are going to do. Your will be done. Amen."

When the technician developed the X-ray film and held it up to view, he looked puzzled. I asked him what the problem was. The answer was, "The X-rays didn't turn out—I'll have to take a new set."

The second set was no different. When Dr. Wieman came in to take a look at them, he put them in a viewer and flipped on the light. *There was new white bone where a black hole had been!* Dr. Wieman said, "I see it, but I don't believe it so I'm going to put you back into a cast."

My response: "I believe it. There is still a God who heals."

It *was* healed, but it would take five long years before my left wrist regained its full strength.

The turning point

Dr. Wieman now sent me to Oregon's Rehabilitation Center in Portland. Upon arriving in Portland, a nurse locked up my sleep-inducing "bombs" and directed me to use instead sedative tranquilizers that were prescribed by the resident doctor. They worked—but instead kept me awake all night. Next night, the same. That next weekend, at the house of some friends, I poured down a toilet all one hundred tranquilizers. I was free at last from my addiction to the "bombs."

Now came the moment of truth. What on earth could the rehab center do for me that I hadn't already done? As I entered the gym doorway and looked at all the dismembered people, I was almost overcome with waves of sadness and empathy. Simultaneously, as if to mock me, excruciating pain once again assailed my entire body. Suddenly it dawned on me: *I am now one of* them. *Never again will I be able to use my mechanics tools or do all the things I used to do.* In short, I hit bottom—completely forgotten: all the miracles that had brought me this far.

Now my attention shifted away from myself to the small man who was in charge of us. I guess he noticed how fascinated I was by him; he came over to me and said, "You think this is something?" With that, he removed one leg and the opposite arm, and continued as though nothing had changed. Then he stooped down and showed me how he tied his shoes one-handed.

Nothing would ever be the same after that for me. Gone was my despondency. Surely

God had a special place for me somewhere.

Not that it would be easy. For starters, the right arm showed no signs of recovery. In the middle of the night, when I awakened in order to roll over, I first had to search for the paralyzed arm. One night, I was terrified to awake with the paralyzed arm draped over my face. Another time, when I was on a creeper under a car, the paralyzed arm got stuck—and I had a tough time disengaging it.

Testing revealed that the log had driven my shoulder down, breaking my ribs, shattering the scapula, compressing my knees and arches of my feet, stretching the nerves until they severed the arteries and yanked the nerves from my spine, with the rest breaking like a stranded cable throughout my shoulder.

Dr. Slocum of Eugene, Oregon, the father of orthopedic surgery, now came into the picture. The big question being, Could my right arm ever recover? He promptly asked me this one question: "Are you right-handed or are you left-handed?"

I replied, "I used to be—" at which point I was cut off with a loud,

"I didn't ask you what you used to be. I asked you, 'Are you right-handed or are you left-handed?'"

I snapped back, "As any fool can see, I am left-handed!"

The doctor wheeled to leave, but I stopped him, and asked if the arm needed to be amputated.

Dr. Slocum's answer was, "Whenever you are ready."

Surgery took place in short order, and I awoke to little resulting pain and a massive feeling of relief.

With *that* taken care of, next to deal with was the gradually increasing pain in my upper spine. X-rays revealed compression fractures in the thoracic area that caused kyphosis of my spine—T5 and T6 now looked like slices of pie. Dr. Wieman then agreed to corrective surgery.

Following surgery, a full-torso body brace, which clasped my neck, braced my chin, gripped my chest, and extended down to my hips, was installed. The brace proved to be hot, painful, and constantly had to be readjusted.

So what next? When I called the Industrial Accident Insurance office, they studied into my situation, and then agreed to pay for three years of college education.

First of all, before classes began, I had to learn how to write again; and that process was made much more difficult by the body brace and fusion pain. My left wrist was weak and tired easily. Result: I was given an oversized pencil and dot-to-dot tracing book. But within very few minutes of trying to trace letters, pain would force me to stop.

I chose advanced mathematics as my major; and I did so well that the state agreed to pay my fourth year as well.

When Dr. Wieman signed my release papers, he said, "You can either continue taking pills for the phantom pains and be a druggie and hurt—or just hurt. I suggest you just hurt." I took his advice.

Dr. Wieman then said, "Now go out and become my first successful patient." At first, I thought he was kidding me, but later I discovered what he meant by that injunction: almost all his other patients collected insurance for life.

After I began my teaching career, social security disability checks kept coming. When we tried to stop them, the answer was, "You won't make it and we don't want to have to start the paperwork all over again." Charlotte and I decided not to cash them—eventually the checks stopped coming.

Our reason was this: We trusted God to see us through, and our goal was now to give back to society rather than my continuing to be a ward of the state.

We moved to Texas and put down roots in Keene. I earned a master's degree in education from Tarleton State University, classes all taken at night. My teaching career in the Keene Independent School District spanned thirty-three years of teaching, administration, and working with church youth groups.

Each year, for twenty-three years now, I have led church mission trips down into Mexico. Almost eerily, the pain I have had to continually live with never ceases—*except*—during those mission trips, miraculously, it stops.

God has been so good.

SECTION FOUR

WHATEVER YOU DO, DO WELL.
FOR WHEN YOU GO TO THE GRAVE,
THERE WILL BE NO WORK OR PLANNING
OR KNOWLEDGE OR WISDOM.
—ECCLESIASTES 9:10, NLT

The impossible—the very word carries a sub-meaning: Don't even attempt such a thing! For you will, absolutely will, fail. I remember such a fork in my life's road: do more research and writing so that my doctoral dissertation would entitle me to a PhD after my name. OR—ridiculous thought!—go on without any extra remuneration, even if it takes years of extra work to get there . . . and thereby become the world's foremost authority on the subject. I took the second road, and never since then have I feared attempting the impossible.

The Countess and the Impossible

Author Unknown

No one in our Utah town knew where the Countess had come from; her carefully precise English indicated that she was not a native American. From the size of her house and staff we knew she must be wealthy, but she never entertained and she made it clear that when she was at home she was completely inaccessible. Only when she stepped outdoors did she become at all a public figure—and then chiefly to the small fry of the town, who lived in awe of her.

The Countess always carried a cane, not only for support but as a means of chastising any youngster she thought needed disciplining. And at one time or another most of the kids in our neighborhood seemed to display that need. By running fast and staying alert I had managed to keep out of her reach. But one day when I was thirteen, as I was short-cutting through her hedge, she got close enough to rap my head with her stick.

"Ouch!" I yelled, jumping a couple of feet.

"Young man, I want to talk to you," she said. I was expecting a lecture on the evils of trespassing, but as she looked at me, half-smiling, she seemed to change her mind. "Don't you live in that green house with the willow trees in the next block?"

"Yes, Ma'am."

"Do you take care of your lawn? Water it? Clip it? Mow it?"

"Yes, Ma'am."

"Good. I've lost my gardener. Be at my house Thursday morning at seven, and don't tell me you have something else to do; I've seen you slouching around on Thursdays."

When the Countess gave an order it was carried out. I didn't dare not come on that next Thursday. I went over the whole lawn three times with a mower before she was satisfied, and then she had me down on all fours looking for weeds until my knees were as green as the grass. She finally called me up to the porch.

"Well, young man, how much do you

want for your day's work?"

"I don't know. Fifty cents maybe."

"Is that what you figure you're worth?"

"Yes'm. About that."

"Very well then. Here's the fifty cents you say you're worth, and here's the dollar and a half more that I've earned for you by pushing you. Now I'm going to tell you something about how you and I are going to work together. There are as many ways of mowing a lawn as there are people, and they may be worth anywhere from a penny to five dollars. Let's say that a three-dollar job would be just what you've done today, except that you would do it all by yourself. A four-dollar job would be so perfect that you'd have to be something of a fool to spend that much time on a lawn. A five-dollar lawn is—well, it's impossible, so we'll forget about that. Now then, each week I'm going to pay you according to your own evaluation of your work."

I left with my two dollars, richer than I remembered being in my whole life, and determined that I would get four dollars out of her the next week. But I failed to reach even the three-dollar mark. My will began faltering the second time around the yard.

"Two dollars again, eh? That kind of job puts you right on the edge of being dismissed, young man."

"Yes'm. But I'll do better next week."

And somehow I did. The last time around

the lawn I was exhausted, but I found I could spur myself on. In the exhilaration of that new feeling I had no hesitation in asking the Countess for three dollars.

Each Thursday for the next four or five weeks I varied between a three and a three-and-a-half dollar job. The more I became acquainted with her lawn, places where the ground was a little high or a little low, places where it needed to be clipped short or left long on the edges to make a more satisfying curve along the garden the more aware I became of just what a four dollar lawn would consist of. And each week I would resolve to do just that kind of job. But by the time I had made my three or three-and-a-half-dollar mark I was too tired to remember ever having had the ambition to go beyond that point.

"You look like a good, consistent three-fifty man," she would say as she handed me the money.

"I guess so," I would say, too happy at the sight of the money to remember that I had shot for something higher.

"Well, don't feel too bad," she would comfort me. "After all, there are only a handful of people in the world who could do a four-dollar job."

And her words were a comfort at first. But then, without my noticing what was happening, her comfort became an irritant that made me resolve I could see myself expiring on her lawn, with the Countess leaning over me, handing me the four dollars with a tear in her eye, begging my forgiveness for having thought I couldn't do it.

It was in the middle of such a fever, one Thursday night when I was trying to forget that day's defeat and get some sleep, that the truth hit me so hard I sat upright, half choking in my excitement. It was the *five-dollar job* I had to do, not the four-dollar one! I had to do the job that no one could do because it was impossible.

I was well acquainted with the difficulties ahead. I had the problem, for example, of doing something about the worm mounds in the lawn. The Countess might not even have noticed them yet, they were so small; but in my bare feet I knew about them and had to do something about them. And I could go on trimming the garden edges with shears, but I knew that a five-dollar lawn demanded that I line up each edge exactly with a yardstick and then trim it precisely with the edger. And there were other problems that only I and my bare feet knew about.

I started the next Thursday by ironing out the worm mounds with a heavy roller. After two hours of that I was ready to give up for the day. Nine o'clock in the morning and my will was already gone! It was only by accident that I discovered how to regain it. Sitting under a walnut tree for a few minutes after finishing the rolling, I fell asleep. When I woke up minutes later the lawn looked so good through my fresh eyes and felt so good under my feet that I was anxious to get on with the job.

I followed this secret for the rest of the day, dozing a few minutes every hour to regain my perspective and replenish my strength. Between naps I mowed four times lengthwise, two times across, until the lawn looked like a green velvet checkerboard. Then I dug around every tree, crumbling the clods and smoothing the soil with my hands, then finished with the edger, meticulously lining up each stroke so the effect would be perfectly symmetrical. And I carefully trimmed the grass between the flagstones of the front walk. The shears wore my fingers raw, but the walk never looked better.

Finally, about eight o'clock that evening, after I had run home at five for a bite of supper, it was all completed. I was so proud I didn't even feel tired when I went up to her door.

"Well, what is it today?" she asked.

"Five dollars," I said, trying for a little calm and sophistication.

"*Five dollars?* You mean four dollars, don't you? I told you that a five-dollar lawn isn't possible."

"Yes it is. I just did it."

"Well, young man, the first five-dollar lawn in history certainly deserves some looking around."

We walked about the lawn together in the last light of evening, and even I was quite overcome by the impossibility of what I had done.

"Young man," she said, putting her hand on my shoulder, "what on earth made you do such a crazy, wonderful thing?"

I didn't know why, but even if I had, I could not have explained it in the excitement of hearing that I had done it.

"I think I know," she continued, "how you felt when this idea came to you of mowing a lawn that I told you was impossible. It made you very happy when it first came, then a little frightened. Am I right?"

She could see she was right by the startled look on my face.

"I know how you felt because the same thing happens to almost everybody. They feel this sudden burst in them wanting to do some great thing. They feel this wonderful happiness. But then it passes because they have said, 'No, I can't do that. It's impossible.' Whenever something in you says 'It's impossible,' remember to take a careful look. See if it isn't really God asking you to grow an inch or a foot or a mile that you may come to a fuller life."

She folded my hand around the money. "You've been a great man today. It's not often a man gets paid for a thing like greatness. You're lucky and I like you. Now run along."

Since that time, some twenty-five years ago, when I have felt myself at an end with nothing before me, suddenly, with the appearance of that word "impossible," I have experienced inside me, and known, that the only possible way lay through the very middle of the impossible.

To see ourselves as others see us—that's what this story is all about. Not easy since each of us looks at ourselves through rose-tinted glasses (thus guaranteeing each of us one enthusiastic admirer).

Consequently, it often takes rather strong medicine to cure the patient in this respect—such as that administered in this story.

Janice was a chronic borrower. She was no respecter of mine and thine. Then when any portion of her wardrobe needed replenishing, or if she lacked any one of the numerous essentials so needful in the everyday life of a boarding school girl, she helped herself to those of her roommate or any one of the forty girls living in Birch Hall of Beverly Academy.

She was very sweet about borrowing. "Oh Helen!" she exclaimed, looking ruefully at the sheer silk stocking in her hand. "My best pair of good ones, and a horrid run right in front! Could you—would you be so kind as to lend me a pair just until after Sabbath? I'll return them none the worse for the loan."

They had to be asked for a week later, and then they were not worth the returning. And so it was—dresses, shoes, hats, gloves, sportswear; to say nothing of the countless miscellaneous odds and ends that were always in demand. However, one found it almost impossible to resist her charming personality, especially when she pleaded so adorably. She was really a sweet girl with many worthy qualities, but every one of her good points were offset by this one big fault. Jan's friends all liked her; but when a girl saw her new sport dress, borrowed unbeknown to its owner, walking into chapel, she could hardly suppress the rising feeling of indignation. Of course, Janice meant to ask permission always, and at first she did ask before appropriating for her personal use the property of another. But as she became more intimately acquainted with the girls, she gradually became bolder, and often availed herself of their possessions without their permission, excusing herself by thinking that they surely would not mind.

"Why, just imagine," exclaimed Helen, "how I felt this morning when I saw my new apple-green suit that I have worn but twice, walking into class on the person of none other than the Janice Redding. Really, I can overlook a number of things, but I do think there is a limit to one's generosity."

"I know it," chimed in Madge. "My manicure set has wandered away, and I haven't seen my shoe polish for a week. I just know Jan has them."

"And I am reduced to the pitiful state of two pairs of hose. Jan borrowed the others, and I had eight pairs at least," this was from Sue, in a plaintive voice.

"We all agree that something emphatic should be done, and yet we are obliged to admit that Janice does have an irresistible personality. Now what can we really do about it?" queried Helen.

"Surely we all know she is very sweet, and that's the simple reason why it will be hard to help her see her fault without hurting her feelings."

The girls looked thoughtfully at each other, trying to think of some plan that could be used, when suddenly—

"Eureka! Girls, I have thought of it!" This came from Barbara, who was noted for her spontaneous outbursts of speech.

"A thought—just imagine," murmured Louise.

"We all know," continued Barbara, completely ignoring the last remark, "what the game 'tit for tat' is, don't we? Let's play something of the sort with Jan. Considering the fact that she does help herself indiscriminately to our belongings, we could return the compliment for a time, and she may come to real-ize our motive for doing it."

"That truly is an idea, Barbara, and a good one at that. I'm for trying it out. How about the rest of you?" asked Sue.

There was an emphatic chorus of "Ayes."

"First," suggested Barbara, "I am going to saunter casually into Jan's room and beg for the use of that new camera she got for her birthday. Then each of you in the next day or two borrow something that she will actually need or miss."

Having decided this, the group dispersed and Barbara went off in the direction of Janice's room. As she reached the door, she paused a minute and listened to the words of the school song sounding out in Jan's sweet soprano. Barbara found herself wishing that she might borrow permanently for her own the birdlike voice. As she stood there with her hand on the door knob, she almost weakened and turned back. But on second thought she decided to carry out the plan. So putting on a nonchalant manner, she knocked and was invited to "come in."

"Hello, Barbara. Make yourself comfortable. Aren't you lost, though, way up here on fourth floor?"

"Thanks, Jan," answered Barbara, sinking into the proffered chair. "No, I can't say that I am lost, but I was in the parlor for a few minutes, and just thought I would make a fashionable visit. By the way, is that your new folding camera?" indicating one that lay on the desk.

"Yes, Uncle Charlie gave it to me for my birthday. Isn't it a beauty?"

"I should say so! My, I'd love to use it this afternoon, if you don't mind. A few of us are going on a hike, and I'm sure we can get fine pictures with it. Thanks, a lot, Jan; I'll be sure to return it this evening," said Barbara, picking up the camera and leaving.

Janice stared at the disappearing of her classmate in wide-eyed amazement. Her brand-new autograph camera that had never been used before, and with a new roll of film already in it! She had been about to refuse graciously explaining that she had planned on using it herself that afternoon, when Barbara, without waiting for a reply, had hurried off with the prized possession.

Madge ran in about fifteen minutes before supper with her wavy blond hair hanging over her shoulders.

"Jan, dear, would you be as kind as you are sweet and let me have a few bobby pins? I have only two left, and I must be ready in time for supper."

"Why, of course, Madge, I haven't so many myself, but you are welcome to a few, I am sure."

"Thank you, Janice; I know you wouldn't desert a friend in need." And Madge helped herself to a generous handful of hairpins, leaving but a very few.

Janice looked at the remains in her tray, and wondered how, with the scanty number left, she would be able to roll her hair up in the new style Sue had shown her, for the reception scheduled for next Saturday night. In thinking about the reception, she wondered if her new dress was suitable for this momentous occasion, so taking it from the closet, she held it up in front of her and scrutinized it critically.

"It is pretty," she said to herself, "and the slippers and scarf harmonize with it perfectly."

She had just returned them carefully to their place and closed the closet door, when Sue burst into the room, disregarding the formality of knocking.

"O—Jan, I'm just on my way to town, and I must have a scarf from you to wear with this suit. You won't mind if I borrow this lovely lavender one of yours, will you?"

"Why, that's my newest," began Janice slowly as Sue took the scarf from its tissue paper wrappings.

"Oh, that's all right, Janice. I'll take immaculate care of it, and it couldn't match my suit better, could it?" And with a "see you later," she was gone.

That evening just before study bell rang, Janice chanced to meet Barbara in the lower hall, and tried to be very casual about her camera.

"Your camera?" asked Barbara with a quizzical expression on her face. "Oh, yes, Jan, I did borrow your camera, didn't I? Now come to think of it I don't recall seeing it since we had our lunch at the Three Pines. I wonder, could I have possibly left it there in the woods? I'm sorry, Jan! I should have been more careful, and there was a shower about an hour ago too." Then noticing the look of anxiety and consternation that showed plainly on the other's face, she reproached herself for being so cruel, knowing all the while that the camera was reposing safely in her bookcase, and had been ever since she first took it. "It will surely turn up all right, Jan," she added; "so don't worry, please."

After two days of strenuous borrowing, Barbara called the girls together and each reported that she had borrowed at least one article from Janice, some with permission and some without.

"Now, Barb," began Helen, "as you seem to have been the instigator of this whole affair, how are we going to bring events to a climax? Or in other words, how are we going to make Jan see the point? We don't want to keep this borrowing up forever—it's getting on my nerves already."

"We could come right out and tell her," suggested Sue.

"No, I don't think that would do at all. We must show more tact than that," replied Madge.

"Yes, let's be tactful by all means," advised Virginia. "Why wouldn't tomorrow night be a good opportunity to 'cap the climax' as Helen has already mentioned?"

"Tomorrow night! We couldn't do anything then. Have you forgotten the reception?"

"That's just it. The reception will make it easy for us. Let's array ourselves in the borrowed apparel that we have and drop in to see her just before time for the doings," finished Virginia.

"All right; leave it to us to work it out successfully, if not triumphantly."

The following evening, about an hour before the appointed time for the reception, Louise stopped at Jan's room and was much surprised to find Jan breathlessly taking off her hat and coat.

"Aren't you going to the reception tonight, Jan? I'm afraid you will have to hustle if you're ready in time."

"Yes, I shall, but you see I just this minute got here. At the eleventh hour I remembered I didn't have enough bobby pins, so had to run over to the store for them. Luckily I have everything ready to step into." So saying she opened the closet door and reached for her new gown. The look of incredulous amazement mingled with that of vexation which spread over her face caused Louise to ask what was the trouble.

"Why, my dress—my new reception dress! I can't find it—and my slippers aren't here either!"

Searching frantically everywhere in the closet revealed no dress, but brought to light her second best was gone also. Janice jumped up quickly, ran across the hall to her chum's room, and burst in at the door without bothering to knock.

"Virgie, what will I do? I can't find my reception—"

The remaining words froze on her lips as she saw the dress in question gracefully adorning her bosom friend.

"Fits me perfectly, Janice, and I knew you wouldn't mind, for you do have so many dresses that would do for an occasion like this. And," she added rather mischievously, "the slippers pinch a bit, but I guess I can stand them for one night."

Janice was still standing, nonplussed, hardly knowing what to say, but finally blurted out:

"Well, I *do* mind, Virginia! What made you think I would wish to wear an old dress to the reception?"

"I didn't honestly think you would, but I did think that as long as you have had the use of my velvet coat since last recital, you wouldn't mind greatly if I borrowed your dress this once."

Janice was slowly beginning to comprehend. Just then several girls came trooping in, each wearing or carrying some borrowed article of Janice's.

"Tit for tat, Janice. You may have this exquisite lavender scarf of yours in exchange for my blue silk parasol," laughed Sue.

"I'm willing to trade your sewing basket for my manicure set and shoe polish," offered Madge.

"And here's your camera, Jan. It hasn't been out of my room one minute since I borrowed it. May I please have my red sweater in return?" asked Barbara.

So around the circle of girls each had some exchange to be made. Jan's first outraged look had changed to chagrin as she realized the victims of her borrowing were in truth returning "tit for tat."

However, she good-naturedly admitted that the "punishment fitted the crime," and that she had not realized such an unfortunate habit had grown to be part of her.

"I must confess, though," she added, "that I certainly was mystified at the sudden popularity of so many of my belongings. Still—it certainly took me a long time to get the idea of your little plan. But though the medicine was strong, I believe it has worked! I'm sure I'm cured!"

"And we're sure, too, Jan dear," chorused her friends.

I've lived a long and rewarding life. Most of the things I've done and said, I've long since forgotten. But I've not forgotten the morning I abused my authority as a junior camp counselor by suggesting we run through a spat line the camper who was always last to make his bed, last to clean his part of the cabin—costing us coveted Best-Cabin honors time after time. So we ran him through. He didn't whimper—but the look of broken-hearted reproach he sent my way has haunted my dreams ever since.

Poor Uncle Si

Author Unknown

I shall never forget that bright, sunny afternoon, when my father stood looking down at us, my two brothers and me.

We had been planning, with great glee, how we would dress up some dark night, and in the character of ghosts, frighten a certain timid schoolfellow of ours.

"It will be jolly fun, boys, I can tell you!" I exclaimed, with a shout of laughter at the idea.

"Jolly fun to you, Harry, but what will it be to him?" asked a deep reproachful voice from the doorway, and glancing up, there stood our father, with a pained look on his face.

It was a new idea! It would be fun to us, but what would it be to him, the poor unoffending boy we were planning to frighten cruelly?

We had never thought of that side of the question at all; boys, aye, and men, too, are apt to look at one side only, and that side the one that pleases themselves the most.

Our father stood a moment in thought, and then he came into the room and sat down.

"My sons," he said, "I see the time has come for me to tell you a story of the long ago, when I was a boy, so full of life and fun that, like you, I did not stop to think whether my fun might not be just the opposite to someone else."

He paused awhile, and a sad, pained shadow crept over his face, a look I had often seen there, and learned to connect with a certain man who dwelt in a little cottage nearby.

He was a large, strong man, about our father's age, but alas! the light of his life, his reason, had gone out forever; he was gentle and harmless, and for the most part cheerful and playful, but there were times when he would fall prone on the floor, quivering with terror, and shrieking out wild appeals to be saved from the ghosts that were about to seize him.

My father often visited this poor fellow, "poor Uncle Si," we boys called him, and on a few occasions he had taken me, his eldest boy, with him; he never went with empty hands, but always carried some little gift, a picture book, candy, cake, or a toy; and even at such times I noted that weary, sad expression creep over my father's usually cheerful face, and remain there, like a cloud, long after our return home. I knew, too, that it was he who, with my Uncle John's assistance, paid the rent of the poor man's cottage, clothed him, and provided for the old woman who took care of him.

And sorely had all this puzzled me, for I knew that "Uncle Si" was in no wise related to my father or mother, and that the money expended in his support could ill be spared for that purpose.

Often my father had promised to tell me the story "when the right time should come;" and it had come now, it seemed, for the first words were of "Uncle Si."

"My boys," he said, "I am going now to tell you the story of Uncle Si. When you have heard it, you will know why I think it my duty to tell it to you just now. I would give ten years of my life if I had no such story to tell. But it is my cross, and one of my own making, so I must bear it patiently as my punishment.

"When I was a boy going to school, there was among my mates a bright little fellow, a good scholar, but a very nervous, timid boy. His mother was a poor woman, who worked hard to support herself and him, and it was

her greatest ambition to see him win his way upward in the world.

"We all liked Silas, he was so gentle; but at the same time, we took advantage of his good temper and his timid nature, and were always playing jokes on him.

"His mother was an Irish woman, and was full of queer superstitions. There seemed nothing too marvelous for her to credit, and Silas had inherited this superstitious tendency in a great degree.

"We boys soon found out his weakness, and nothing pleased us more than after the afternoon session was over, to sit on the schoolhouse steps and vie with each other in inventing the most outrageous and startling stories of ghosts, robbers, and murderers. Si would listen, with his blue eyes almost starting from their sockets, and his cheeks turning white and red, finally becoming excited to such a pitch that he would jump at every sudden noise, the slamming of a door or the stamping of a foot on the pavement.

"One afternoon we had been indulging in our favorite amusement until the sun had almost gone down, and darkness began to steal softly across the fields and woods around us.

" 'Oh, what shall I do!' exclaimed Silas, looking fearfully around. 'I must go over to Farmer Brown's, and it will be dark before I can get home.'

" 'To Farmer Brown's!' said I, winking at

the other boys; 'then you'll have to cross the old bridge over Long Pond, Si, and they say that the ghost of the woman who drowned herself there haunts it after nightfall; that's only on the anniversary of her death, though, so—but I say, boys, what day of the month is this?'

" 'The tenth,' was the answer.

"I drew in my lips in a long whistle, and looked hard at Silas.

" 'Then I'm glad I don't have to go that way tonight,' I muttered in a low tone, yet not so low but that he heard me, as I meant he should.

" 'Why, why?' he stammered, turning white as a sheet; 'is it—'

" 'Yes, it is, since you must know. But do not be afraid, old fellow, I don't believe the story anyhow. Who ever heard of a ghost with fiery ribs and fiery spots all over his face? Pshaw, it's all humbug.'

"But poor Silas was thoroughly alarmed; indeed, I intended he should be, and thought his terror fine sport, or rather the beginning of some fine sport, for I had made up a plan of which this was only the prelude.

"While Silas hesitated, divided between the fear of meeting the ghost and the certainty of a whipping if he did not perform his errand, I called my brother John aside and in a hurried whisper told him of my plan, which we decided to keep to ourselves.

"As a result, John proposed to accompany Silas on his errand, an offer the poor fellow gratefully accepted, and so they set off together, and the rest of our party started for home.

"I made some excuse to turn off before I reached my own home, and ran with all speed to the drug store, where I bought a stick of phosphorus; then I darted home, and succeeded in getting possession of a small sheet, and in slipping off again unnoticed.

"Very soon I found myself at the bridge, and there, hidden behind a bush, I proceeded to trace over my dark jacket the outline of skeleton ribs; and very startling they looked,— the white, glowing lines shining out clear and distinct through the darkness, for by this time it was entirely dark. Then I put some of the phosphorus on my hands and face, and wrapped the sheet around my waist, leaving it to trail behind me.

"Thus prepared, I posted myself a few yards beyond the bridge, on the side the boys would reach first on their return path.

"Soon, I heard Silas's voice.

" 'Oh John, I'm afraid, I'm afraid.'

" 'Nonsense,' answered my brother. 'The idea of a ghost! I'd like to see one.'

" 'Oh, don't, don't say that. Oh, o-h!'

"Such a cry of intense, utter horror I hope never to hear again; and as Silas uttered it, he fell all in a heap on the ground. John, according to our agreement, shrieked also and started to run, as if terribly frightened. An instant Silas lay there, and my heart gave a great leap. Was he dead? Had I killed him? But no, my boys, I had done nothing so merciful as that.

"Silas sprang to his feet again, and uttering shriek after shriek, rushed headlong down the road toward the bridge. By this time, seeing how terribly in earnest he was, I began to think that my fun had gone quite far enough, so I followed at full speed, calling out to him that it was all a joke and no ghost at all.

"But he never heeded a word I uttered; on and on he ran, shrieking all the way, until he reached the bridge, and there, to my horror, he sprang with one leap over the wall down into the soft, slimy mud and water at the margin of the pond.

"John had turned back, and tearing loose the sheet from around my waist, I rushed with him down the steep bank to the spot where Silas was. There was more mud than water just there, as we well knew, and the force of his descent had sent him down into the deep, yielding slime, until only his head and shoulders were above the surface, and to our further alarm we saw that he was slowly sinking down, down, down.

"Something must be done, and that speedily, or he would be buried alive before our eyes. Some heavy planks were lying on the shore, and seizing those we dragged them out into the mud until we had formed a line reaching to the spot where poor Silas was still shrieking, 'The ghost! the ghost! the ghost!'

"How we two boys contrived to drag him out of that oozing slime I cannot understand. But we did it somehow, and between us we got him back home, though he broke away from us several times with the old cry of 'The ghost!'

"He was very ill for weeks after that, and when his body got well the doctors said his mind would never come back again, and from that time to this he has been just as you see him now.

"As long as his unhappy mother lived, your Uncle John and I helped her to take care of him, and ever since her death, long years ago, we have entirely supported the miserable victim of our cruel 'fun,' though it was more my sin than your uncle's, for I was the ringleader.

"My sons, that piece of thoughtless 'fun' has saddened my whole life and clouded its brightest moments."

Father ended his story, and sat looking down at our awestruck faces as we murmured in sorrowful tones, "Poor Uncle Silas!"

"Well, my sons," he said after a while, "I am waiting to hear what that plan is that it will be such fun to play off on Sam Harrow."

We hung our heads in silence, and he smiled gently.

"Ah, I see you know why I have told you my sad story today. You have read its lesson. And now, boys, I can trust you, I know; but lest you might forget, I want each of you to lay his hand on this Holy Book, and remembering that our Father in heaven is listening to you, promise never to indulge in any sport that may injure or distress your fellow creatures."

And then, standing at our dear father's knee, we each gave a solemn pledge that we have never broken, and our lives have been the better and happier for it.

As I walked the hallways of the hospital hour after hour, desperately hoping I could make it through the night without pancreatic sword-thrusts that would accelerate my passing, about 1:00 A.M., I struck up a conversation with a woman in the break room who told me she was there to watch over her husband who had a virulent form of leukemia. She'd been by his side for twenty-five years. "He can't even turn over without me," she said.

"My dear woman!" I responded. "How do you do it?" I'll never forget her answer:

"The Lord gives me strength for . . . one day at a time."

Just as was true with Beth in this story, my life has never been the same since talking with someone suffering far more than I was.

QUIET ZONE

Alma Mager Campbell

I wonder what it will be like?" Beth mused as the monotonous whir of the bus wheels beneath her echoed the word so firmly lodged in her mind, "Lonely, lonely, lone—ly." She was on her way to the hospital to spend Christmas Day in preparation for her operation scheduled for December 26.

As the bus stopped at Walnut and Second Street, she moved closer to the window to look at the street sign. Almost involuntarily she put her coat collar up to shut out the inevitable whiff of cold that would come in when the door would be opened to discharge three waiting girls. Although she saw the everyday world of people, stores, and office buildings enchantingly disguised by the Midas touch of the setting sun, she shivered slightly.

It was a gorgeous storybook evening—Christmas Eve. Cheer abounded everywhere. Fragments of carols wafted through the air. High and clear above the noise of the city's streets the church bells chimed. Such surroundings merely accentuated the bleakness in Beth's heart.

"It's only minor surgery," she reminded herself. It was, as far as risk was concerned, but it was surgery for a handicap that had made her extremely self-conscious. She had a cleft palate, with its accompanying impediment of speech, and her upper lip needed plastic surgery.

Like any other girl, Beth wanted to be attractive in the eyes of her friends and companions. She dreaded, too, the way people frequently asked her to repeat conversation because they couldn't understand what she had said. Perhaps the operation would help; perhaps it wouldn't. Despite the happiness around her, she was no part of that merry city. It lay wrapped now in the haze of dusk and tied together with myriad gleaming lights, like some huge cellophane-taped package waiting to be opened by a starry-eyed child. Beth's spirit was that of a forsaken orphan whose holiday stocking was hanging hopelessly limp before an empty fireplace.

How she dreaded to have the bus arrive at her stop, for she was timid about entering the hospital alone, even though all arrangements had been made. Beth's stepmother was kept much too occupied with the younger children to leave home for only a short time. Her father, of course, was busy with his work, so there was no one to accompany her on this first visit to a hospital. She was sixteen, and "old enough to be doing for herself"; so she had been told.

The hiss of the air brakes cut the girl's meditations short. Quickly she scanned the street corner. This was it. Rising from her seat, she buzzed the driver, afraid he might start the bus before she reached the door. Hurriedly she picked up her shabby overnight bag, walked to the front of the bus, and seconds later, was standing on the street corner.

For a moment she watched the blinking red lights on the back of the disappearing bus. Then she turned her head reluctantly to look over her shoulder at the hospital building that towered above her, at lighted windows staring at her like so many inquiring eyes. She almost wished that the building would disappear, that she would awaken in her own bed only to find she had been dreaming.

"Come, Beth, where's your courage," she whispered to herself. For a moment she thought of praying, but dismissed the idea.

Beth was ashamed to ask God anything. It was almost a year since she had been inside the little church on Greenwood Street. You don't ignore Someone and then suddenly ask Him a favor. No doubt, too, He had forgotten her.

Resolutely she grasped her bag in her left hand and started up the concrete sidewalk to the hospital. Although she had only twelve steps to climb to the entrance, she felt as though she had a ten-pound weight on each foot and was trying to reach the top of Mount Everest. At last she was at the door. No need to ring or knock—or whatever one did at a place like that—for a pleasant-faced nurse on her way off duty greeted her and held the door open to let her in.

Once inside the lobby, Beth tiptoed toward the information desk just opposite the doorway. Trying to gain courage to speak, she cleared her throat. The girl at the desk looked up, "Can I help you?"

"I'm Elizabeth Bates."

"Oh, you were scheduled to come in this evening. You are right on time. I'll ring for a nurse to show you to your ward," was the crisp, efficient greeting. Those few words made Beth feel somewhat better. She rose from her gloomy thoughts, straightened her hat, and managed to step right along behind the chipper woman who ushered her into an elevator. An instant later the door clicked, and Beth stepped out on the third floor, where another crisp personality took charge of her.

For an hour or more the new patient was so busy being whisked from one hospital routine to another that she had no time for the doldrums. Finally she was ready for bed. Since she shared the ward with about twenty other guests, she began to look around.

The convalescing woman in the next bed introduced herself. Beth in turn explained as well as she could why she herself was there. The woman nodded understandingly, and in an aside she whispered, "I want you to go over there and visit that girl." She motioned in the direction of the left corner of the room.

Although Beth was not in the mood for social overtures, she moved slowly toward the bed the woman had indicated. Never would she forget that moment. In the upper half of the bed lay a wee mound covered with a great white Sahara of bedclothes stretching away on all sides. At first glance Beth thought the occupant was a child. Then the little hump moved and a husky voice scarcely above a whisper said, "Hello. Nice place to spend Christmas, isn't it? Merry Christmas anyway."

Beth was so totally unprepared for what she saw and heard that she just stood there. "I guess you wonder who I am," the voice went on. "Well, I'm a girl, too, a little older than you perhaps, but I'm young too. I know I don't look it, but I am. My name is Marva James."

By that time Beth, who had recovered at least partially from her astonishment, tried to say something. "The woman in the next bed to me told me to come to see you," she managed.

"She's always sending me customers. You see, I sell cheer. You need a little?"

Beth felt somewhat confused. *I should be handing out the cheer to her*, she was thinking, but she replied, "I could use some, I suppose."

"Not feeling sorry for yourself, are you?"

Beth wanted to say no by this time. Being a very honest person, she answered, "I'm afraid I was just saturated with self-pity when I entered this place tonight."

"I thought so," said the little hump in the bed (then Beth couldn't believe her ears—a chuckle—a mischievous chuckle), "until you saw me. Don't mind me; I'm used to these surroundings. This is my hotel. I've been here before, many times. I've also had two operations, and I'm waiting for a third."

"Not major ones, I hope," offered Beth.

"Yes, major ones. This one is my last chance. You see, since childhood I've been terribly crippled with arthritis. I've hardly known what it is like to be without pain, especially these last three years, but God has helped me bear the suffering. I try to repay His merciful kindness by cheering others in any way that I can. I am totally helpless. I can't even feed myself."

Pushing the covers aside with a movement of her shoulders, she showed Beth her hands, crippled and distorted beyond recognition. In her early years she had been able to walk or crawl short distances. Now someone had to carry her from place to place or move her in a wheelchair.

That conversation transformed Beth's whole outlook. *Just what is my tiny handicap compared with this girl's suffering?* she thought. *I should be thoroughly ashamed of myself, and I am.*

Beth's evening passed almost pleasantly. Mrs. Tate, the woman in the next bed, explained the procedures usually followed in preparing patients for surgery. Somehow the revealing of the unknown made Beth feel better. That night for the first time in a long while she breathed a little prayer before going to sleep.

The next day was ushered in for Beth with a cheery voice saying, "Merry Christmas! Let's put this in your mouth," and she felt the slender glass tube under her tongue. The routine of temperature reading, pulse taking, and baths was soon over. Before she knew it, the new patient was dressed in her robe and seated in a chair actually enjoying her breakfast.

The day, with its excellent dinner, visitors, and cheery atmosphere, passed by quickly. She had spent the afternoon by Marva's bedside. Each girl had told the other about her family, her friends, and the trivia that interest most girls.

The next morning Beth was wheeled into the operating room. Seconds later, so it seemed to her, she opened her eyes, and a nurse beside her bed said, "Well, it's all over."

As soon as the soreness in Beth's mouth and throat subsided, she was up and around, spending much time beside Marva's bed. The acquaintance of the two girls ripened into a real friendship. Though Beth's operation did not entirely correct her handicap, she left the hospital a new person in many ways, for she had shared the confidence of a courageous soul.

When Marva was dismissed from the hospital she knew that she was going home to die. The third operation had not been attempted because her disease had advanced too far. About a month after leaving the hospital Beth visited the crippled girl in her home, and continued doing so until the time of her death three months later. Each time she went Beth wondered whether Marva would be there to greet her. That the crippled girl never shrank from the thought of her fate made Beth marvel. During one of the visits close to the time of her death, Marva revealed to her friend something about which Beth had wondered but had never had the courage to ask.

"You know, Beth," she said, "I am sure you wonder why I can take this. Nobody young wants to die. I am suffering, and, of course, I don't like the pain I have to bear. I know that when the end comes I shall have peace, eternal peace. I know, too, it is God's will. Why, I do not know; I'm leaving that to Him. I don't feel sorry for myself. I have never wanted pity, nor do I want it now. Truly, I believe that if I had to live my twenty-one years over again just this way, I'd be willing to do it, so firmly do I believe God has His plans and purposes.

"I have many friends, some of whom I have helped. Thinking of others has made life not only bearable but even pleasant at times, and I do thank God for all the things I have enjoyed despite my pain."

That revelation helped Beth to grow up. She suddenly realized how ingrown her thinking had been, how she had been constantly preoccupied with pity for herself and her own troubles, with never a thought for others and their difficulties. She saw clearly that she had forsaken God; He had not forsaken her.

Gradually into her heart came the desire to renew her faith, that she might have One to share with others.

One Sabbath about a year after Marva's death Beth put on her best clothes and started for church. The sunshine of the Sabbath morning flooded her soul and peace entered her heart as once again her shadow fell across the threshold of God's house. The words of the wise man, "In all thy ways acknowledge him, and he shall direct thy paths" (Proverbs 3:6, KJV), took on richer and deeper significance for her.

The signpost on Beth's path pointed to a Christian academy, where she spent two and a half happy years. Today she is enrolled in the prenursing course at Glenview College, where her cheery smile and genial personality have won her many friends. Her way has not been without some thorns, but she believes she is learning under God's tutelage.

This past summer Beth underwent two more operations on her throat, one in July and one in September. Slowly her affliction is yielding to the surgeon's efforts. She has two more ordeals to meet before total recovery can be achieved. Each time she mounts the hospital steps she thinks of Marva. Each time she thanks God for His healing power and prays that the unselfish spirit of Marva may permeate her soul, that her attention and time may be directed to helping others.

Beth's courage shines like new armor as she begins her second year of college work. She envisages the day when she will become a "lady with the lamp." As she serves the sick she hopes to follow the example of the Great Physician who said, "Whether is easier, to say, Thy sins be forgiven thee; or to say, Arise, and walk?" (Matthew 9:5, KJV).

*I*t wasn't very long ago when almost every county had a poor house—a last resort when your money ran out. There were no credit cards back then, so you couldn't spend money you didn't have like people do today.

Belatedly, I have come to realize that, in life, one cannot out-give. When you trust in God and seek to do His will and faithfully minister to His sheep—never, will you be left high and dry. God steps in—not, perhaps, with rich handouts but invariably with enough . . . *"just for today."* Christ even urged us to pray for this: *"Give us this day, our daily bread"* (Matthew 6:11, KJV).

At the time this story was written, a ten-dollar gold piece was worth a lot *of money, in today's* purchasing power.

ELNATHAN'S GOLD

Author Unknown

They each were all the other had, the old man of sixty-eight and the boy of twelve. For some time they lived on the old man's gold, but there came a time where the end of it was not far off; then it was that the boy realized that it was time to put another kind of gold to good use.

One morning Christopher Lightenhome, aged sixty-eight, received an unexpected legacy of six hundred dollars. His good old face betokened no surprise, but it shone with a great joy. "I'm never surprised at the Lord's mercies," he said, reverently. Then, with a step to which vigor had suddenly returned, he sought out Elnathan Owsley, aged twelve.

"Elnathan," he said, "I guess I'm the oldest man in the poorhouse, but I feel just about your age. Suppose you and I get out of here."

The boy smiled. He was very old for twelve, even as Christopher Lightenhome was very young for sixty-eight.

"For a poorhouse this is a good place," continued Christopher, still with that jubilant tone in his voice. "It's well conducted, just as the county reports say. Still there are other places that suit me better. You come and live with me, Elnathan. What do you say to it, boy?"

"Where you going to live?" asked Elnathan, cautiously.

The old man regarded him approvingly. "You'll never be one to get out of the frying pan into the fire, will you?" he said. "But I know a room. I've had my eye on it. It's big enough to have a bed, a table, a cookstove, and three chairs in it, and we could live there like lords. Like lords, boy! Just think of it! I can get it for two dollars a month."

"With all these things in it?"

"No, with nothing in it. But I can buy the things, Elnathan. Get them cheap at the second-hand store. And I can cook to beat—well to beat some women anyway." He paused to think a moment of Adelizy, one of the pauper cooks. *Yes*, he thought, *Adelizy has her days. She's systematic. Some days things are all but pickled in brine, and other days she doesn't put in any salt at all. Some days they're overcooked, and other days it seems as if Adelizy jerked them off the stove before they were heated through.* Then he looked eagerly into the unresponsive young face before him. "What's the matter with my plan, Elnathan?" he asked, gravely. "Why don't you fall in with it? I never knew you to hang back like this before."

"I haven't any money," was the slow answer. "I can't do my share toward it. And I'm not going to live off of you. Your money will last you twice as long if you don't have me to keep. Adelizy says six hundred dollars isn't much, if you do think it's a fortune, and you'll soon run through with it and be back here again."

For a moment the old man was stung. "I certainly won't spend most of it for salt to put into my victuals anyway," he said. Then his face cleared, and he laughed. "So you haven't any money, and you won't let me keep you," he continued. "Well, those are pretty honorable objections. I expect to do away with them though, immediately." He drew himself up and said, impressively: " 'That is gold which is worth gold.' You've got the gold all right, Elnathan, or the money, whichever you choose to call it."

Elnathan stared.

"Why, boy, look here!" Mr. Lightenhome exclaimed, as he seized the hard young arm where much enforced toil had developed good muscle. "There's your gold, in that right arm of yours. What you want to do is to get it out of your arm and into your pocket. I don't need to keep you. You can live with me and keep yourself. What do you say now?"

The boy's face was alight. "Let's go today," he said.

"Not today—tomorrow," decided Mr. Lightenhome, gravely. "When I was young, before misfortune met me and I was cheated out of all I had, I was used to giving spreads. We'll give one tonight to those we used to be fellow paupers with no longer ago than yesterday, and tomorrow we'll go. We began this year in the poorhouse, we'll end it in our own home. That's one of the bad beginnings that made a good ending, boy. There's more than one of them. Mind that."

The morrow came, and the little home was started. Another morrow followed, and Elnathan began in earnest to try getting the gold out of his arm and into his pocket. He was a dreamy boy with whom very few had had patience, for nobody, not even himself, knew the resistless energy and dogged perseverance that lay dormant within him. Mr. Lightenhome, however, suspected it. "I believe," he said to himself, "that Elnathan, when he once gets awakened, will be a hustler.

But the poorhouse isn't exactly the place to rouse up the ambition of Napoleon Bonaparte in any boy. Having a chance to scold somebody is what Adelizy calls one of the comforts of a home. And she certainly took out her comforts on Elnathan, and all the rest helped her—sort of deadening to him, though. Living here with me and doing for himself is a little more like what's needed in his case."

Slowly Elnathan awakened, and Mr. Lightenhome had patience with him. He earned all he could, and he kept himself from being a burden on his only friend, but he disliked work, and so he lagged over it, but he did all that he did well, and he was thoroughly trustworthy.

Three years went by. Elnathan was fifteen, and Christopher Lightenhome was seventy-one.

The little room had always been clean. There had been each day enough nourishing food to eat, though the old man, remembering Adelizy's prediction, had set his face like flint against even the slightest indulgence in table luxuries. And although there had been days when Elnathan had recklessly brought home a ten-cent pie and half a dozen doughnuts from the baker's as his share of provision for their common dinner, Mr. Lightenhome felt that he had managed well.

And yet there were only fifty dollars of the original six hundred left, and the poorhouse was looming once more on the old man's sight. He sighed. An expression of patience grew on the kind, old face. He felt it to be a great pity that six hundred dollars could not be made to go farther. And there was a wistfulness in the glance he cast upon the boy. Elnathan was, as yet, only half awake. The little room and the taste of honest independence had done their best. Were they to fail?

The old man began to economize. His mittens wore out. He did not buy more. He needed new flannels, but he did not buy them. Instead he tried to patch the old ones, and Elnathan, coming in suddenly, caught him doing it.

"Why, Uncle Chris!" he exclaimed. "What are you patching those old things for? Why don't you pitch 'em out and get new ones?"

The old man kept silent till he had his needle threaded. Then he said softly, with a half apology in his tone: "The money's 'most gone, Elnathan."

The boy was startled. He knew as well as Mr. Lightenhome that when the last coin was spent, the doors of the poorhouse would open once more to receive his only friend. At the thought a thrill of gladness went through him as he recognized that he himself was safe. He could provide for himself. He need never return. And by that thrill in his own heart he guessed the feeling of his friend. He could not put what he guessed into words. Nevertheless he felt sure that the old man would not falter nor complain.

"How much have you left?" he asked.

Mr. Lightenhome told him.

Then, without a word, Elnathan got up and went out. His head sunk in thought, and his hands in his trousers pockets, he sauntered on in the wintry air while he mentally calculated how long Mr. Lightenhome's funds would last. "Not any later than next spring anyhow," he said at last. "And next Christmas he'll be in the poorhouse again." He walked on a few steps. Then he stopped. "Will he?" he cried. "Not if I know it!"

This was a big resolve for a boy of fifteen, and the next morning Elnathan himself thought so. He thought so even to the extent of considering a retreat from the high task which he had the previous day set for himself. Then he looked at Mr. Lightenhome, who had aged perceptibly in the last hours. Evidently he had lain awake in the night calculating how long his money would last. The sight of him nerved the boy afresh. *I'm not going back on it,* he told himself, vigorously. *I'm just going to dig out all the gold there is in me. Keeping Uncle Chris out of the poorhouse is worth it.*

But he did not confide in the old man. "He'd say it was too big a job for me and talk about how I ought to get myself some school-ing," concluded the boy.

Now it came about that the room, which while it had not been the habitation of lords; had been the abode of kingly kindness, became a silent place. The anxious old man had no heart to joke. He had been to the poorhouse and had escaped from it into freedom. His whole nature rebelled at the thought of returning. And yet he tried to school himself to look forward to it bravely. *If it is the Lord's will,* he told himself, *I'll have to bow to it.*

Meanwhile whose who employed Elnathan were finding him a very different boy from the slow, lagging Elnathan they had known. If he was sent on an errand, he made speed. "Here! Get the gold out of your legs," he would say to himself. If he sprouted potatoes for a grocer in his cellar, "There's gold in your fingers, El," he would say. "Get it out as quick as you can."

He now worked more hours in a day than he had ever worked before, so he was too tired to talk much at meals and too sleepy in the evening. But there was a light in his eyes when they rested on Mr. Lightenhome that made the old man's heart thrill. "Elnathan would stand by me if he could," he would say to himself. "He's a good boy. I must not worry him."

A month after Elnathan had begun his

great labor of love, an astonishing thing happened to him. He had a choice of two places offered him as general utility boy in a grocery store. Once he would have told Mr. Lightenhome, and asked his advice as to which offer he should take, but he was now shouldering his own burdens. He considered carefully, and then he went to Mr. Benson. "Mr. Benson," he said, "Mr. Dale wants me, too, and you both offer the same wages. Now which one of you will give me my groceries reduced as you do your other clerks?"

"I will not," replied Mr. Benson, firmly. "Your demand is ridiculous. You are not a clerk."

The irate Mr. Benson turned on his heel, and Elnathan felt himself dismissed. He then went to Mr. Dale, to whom he honestly related the whole.

Mr. Dale laughed. "But you are not a clerk," he said, kindly.

"I know it, but I mean to be, and I mean to do all I can for you too."

Mr. Dale looked at him, and he liked the bearing of the boy. "Go ahead," he said. "You may have your groceries at the same rate I make for my clerks."

"Thank you," responded Elnathan, while the gratitude he felt crept into his tones. *For myself,* he thought, *I wouldn't have asked for a reduction, but for Uncle Chris I will. I've a big job on hand.*

That day he told Mr. Lightenhome that he had secured a place at Mr. Dale's and that he was to have a reduction on groceries. "Which means, Uncle Chris, that I pay for the groceries for us both while you do the cooking and pay the rent."

Silently and swiftly Mr. Lightenhome calculated. He saw that if he were saved the buying of the groceries for himself, he could eke out his small hoard till after Christmas. The poorhouse receded a little from the foreground of his vision as he gazed into the eyes of the boy opposite him at the table. He did not know that his own eyes spoke eloquently of his deliverance, but Elnathan choked as he went on eating.

"Now hustle, El!" he commanded one day on his way back to the store. "There's gold in your eyes if you keep 'em open and in your tongue if you keep it civil, and in your back and in your wits if they're nimble. All I have to say is, get it out."

"Get it out," he repeated when he had reached the rear of the store. And he began busily to fill and label kerosene cans, gasoline cans, and molasses jugs. From there he went to the cellar to measure up potatoes.

"Never saw such a fellow!" grumbled his companion utility boy. "You'd think he ran the store by the way he steps round with his head up and them sharp eyes of his into everything. 'Hi there!' he said to me. 'Fill that measure of gasoline full before you pour into the can. Mr. Dale doesn't want the name of giving short measure because you're careless.' Let's do some reporting on him, and get him out of the store," he said.

"But there's nothing to report."

But the boy persisted, and very shortly he found himself out of a position.

"You needn't get another boy if you don't want to, Mr. Dale," observed Elnathan, cheerily. "I'm so used to the place now that I can do all he did, as well as my own work. And anyway I'd rather do the extra work than go on watching somebody to keep him from measuring up short or wrong grade on everything he touches." And Elnathan smiled. He had lately discovered that he had ceased to hate work.

Mr. Dale smiled in return. "Very well," he said. "Go ahead and do it all if you want to."

A week he went ahead, and at the end of that time he found, to his delight, that Mr. Dale had increased his wages. "Did you think I would take the work of two boys and pay for the work of one?"

"I didn't think at all, sir," replied Elnathan joyously, "but I'm the gladdest boy in Kingston to get a raise."

"Uncle Chris," he said that night, "I got a raise today."

Mr. Lightenhome expressed his pleasure and his sense that the honor was well merited,

but Elnathan did not hear a word he said because he had something more to say himself. "Uncle Chris," he went on, his face very red, "I've been saving up for some time, and tomorrow's your birthday. Here's a present for you;" and he thrust out a ten-dollar gold piece with the words, "I never gave a present before."

Slowly the old man took the money, and again his eyes outdid his tongue in speaking his gratitude. And there was a great glow in the heart of the boy.

"That's some of the gold I dug out of myself, Uncle Chris," he laughed. "You're the one who first told me it was in me. I don't know whether it came out of my arms or my legs or my head."

"I know where the very best gold there is in you is located, Elnathan," smiled the old man. "It's your heart that is gold, my boy."

Two months later Elnathan was a clerk at fifteen dollars a week. "Now we're fixed, Uncle Chris!" he cried, when he told the news. "You and I can live forever on fifteen dollars a week."

"Do you mean it?" asked the old man, tremblingly. "Do you wish to be encumbered with me?"

"No, I do not, Uncle Chris," answered the boy, with a beaming look. "I don't want to be encumbered with you. I just want to go on living here with you."

Then to the old man the poorhouse forever receded from sight. He remembered Adelizy no more as he looked with pride and tenderness on the boy who stood erect and alert before him; looked again and yet again, for he saw in him the Lord's deliverer, though he knew not he had been raised up by his own kind hand.

*I*t was a gray wintry evening, and his thoughts matched the weather. Then the Old Man took him up to his offices and had him listen to three stories, each with two words which matched his own.

This story reminds me of two lines from one of America's most beloved poets, John Greenleaf Whittier's "Maud Muller":

For of all sad words of tongue or pen
The saddest are these: "It might have been!"

Excerpted from Gordon's best-selling book, A Touch of Wonder.

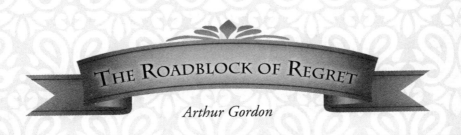

THE ROADBLOCK OF REGRET

Arthur Gordon

Nothing in life is more exciting and rewarding than the sudden flash of insight that leaves you a changed person—not only changed, but changed for the better. Such moments are rare, certainly, but they come to all of us. Sometimes from a book, a sermon, a line of poetry. Sometimes from a friend. . . .

That wintry afternoon in Manhattan, waiting in the little French restaurant, I was feeling frustrated and depressed. Because of several miscalculations on my part, a project of considerable importance in my life had fallen through. Even the prospect of seeing a dear friend (the Old Man, as I privately and affectionately thought of him) failed to cheer me as it usually did. I sat there frowning at the checkered tablecloth, chewing the bitter cud of hindsight.

He came across the street, finally, muffled in his ancient overcoat, shapeless felt hat pulled down over his bald head, looking more like an energetic gnome than an eminent psychiatrist. His offices were nearby; I knew he had just left his last patient of the day. He was close to eighty, but he still carried a full caseload, still acted as director of a large foundation, and still loved to escape to the golf course whenever he could.

By the time he came over and sat beside me, the waiter had brought his invariable drink. I had not seen him for several months, but he seemed as indestructible as ever. "Well, young man," he said without preliminary, "what's troubling you?"

I had long since ceased to be surprised at his perceptiveness. So I proceeded to tell him, at some length, just what was bothering me. With a kind of melancholy pride, I tried to be very honest. I blamed no one else for my disappointment, only myself. I analyzed the whole thing, all the bad judgments, the false moves. I went on for perhaps fifteen minutes, while the Old Man sipped his drink in silence.

When I finished, he put down his glass. "Come on," he said. "Let's go back to my office."

"Your office? Did you forget something?"

"No," he said mildly. "I want your reaction to something. That's all."

A chill rain was beginning to fall outside, but his office was warm and comfortable and familiar: book-lined walls, long leather couch, signed photograph of Sigmund Freud, tape recorder by the window. His secretary had gone home. We were alone.

The Old Man took a tape from a flat cardboard box and fitted it into the machine. "On this tape," he said, "are three short recordings made by three persons who came to me for help. They are not identified, of course. I want you to listen to the recordings and see if you can pick out the two-word phrase that is the common denominator in all three cases." He smiled. "Don't look so puzzled. I have my reasons."

What the owners of the voices on the tape had in common, it seemed to me, was unhappiness. The man who spoke first evidently had suffered some kind of business loss or failure; he berated himself for not having worked harder, for not having looked ahead. The woman who spoke next had never married because of a sense of obligation to her widowed mother; she recalled bitterly all the marital chances she had let go by. The third voice belonged to a mother whose teenage son was in trouble with the police; she blamed herself endlessly.

The Old Man switched off the machine and leaned back in his chair. "Six times in those recordings a phrase is used that's full of a subtle poison. Did you spot it? No? Well, perhaps that's because you used it three times yourself down in the restaurant a little while ago." He picked up the box that had held the tape and tossed it over to me. "There they are, right on the label. The two saddest words in any language."

I looked down. Printed neatly in red ink were the words: "IF ONLY."

"You'd be amazed," said the Old Man, "if you knew how many thousands of times I've sat in this chair and listened to woeful sentences beginning with those two words. '*If only*,' they say to me, 'I had done it differently—or not done it at all. *If only* I hadn't lost my temper, said that cruel thing, made that dishonest move, told that foolish lie. *If only* I had been wiser, or more unselfish, or more self-controlled.' They go on and on until I stop them. Sometimes I make them listen to the recordings you just heard. '*If only*,' I say to them, 'you'd stop saying *if only*, we might begin to get somewhere!' "

The Old Man stretched out his legs. "The trouble with *if only*," he said, "is that it doesn't change anything. It keeps the person facing the wrong way—backward instead of forward. It wastes time. In the end, if you let it become a habit, it can become a real roadblock—an excuse for not trying anymore.

"Now take your own case: Your plans didn't work out. Why? Because you made certain mistakes. Well, that's all right: Everyone makes mistakes. Mistakes are what we learn from. But when you were telling me about them, lamenting this, regretting that, you weren't really learning from them."

"How do you know?" I said, a bit defensively.

"Because," said the Old Man, "you never got out of the past tense. Not once did you mention the future. And in a way—be honest, now!—you were enjoying it. There's a perverse streak in all of us that makes us like to hash over old mistakes. After all, when you relate the story of some disaster or disappointment that has happened to you, you're still the chief character, still in the center of the stage."

I shook my head ruefully. "Well, what's the remedy?"

"Shift the focus," said the Old Man promptly. "Change the key words and substitute a phrase that supplies lift instead of creating drag."

"Do you have such a phrase to recommend?"

"Certainly. Strike out the words *if only*; substitute the phrase *next time*."

"*Next time?*"

"That's right. I've seen it work minor mi-

racles right here in this room. As long as a patient keeps saying *if only* to me, he's in trouble. But when he looks me in the eye and says *next time*, I know he's on his way to overcoming his problem. It means he has decided to apply the lessons he has learned from his experience, however grim or painful it may have been. It means he's going to push aside the roadblock of regret, move forward, take action, resume living. Try it yourself. You'll see."

My old friend stopped speaking. Outside, I could hear the rain whispering against the windowpane. I tried sliding one phrase out of my mind and replacing it with the other. It was fanciful, of course, but I could hear the new words lock into place with an audible click.

"One last thing," the Old Man said. "Apply this little trick to things that can still be remedied." From the bookcase behind him he pulled out something that looked like a diary. "Here's a journal kept a generation ago by a woman who was a schoolteacher in my hometown. Her husband was a kind of amiable ne'er-do-well, charming but a totally inadequate provider. This woman had to raise the children, pay the bills, and keep the family together. Her diary is full of angry references to Jonathan's weaknesses, Jonathan's shortcomings, and Jonathan's inadequacies.

"Then Jonathan died, and all the entries ceased except for one—years later. Here it is: *Today I was made superintendent of schools, and*

I suppose I should be very proud. But if I knew that Jonathan was out there somewhere beyond the stars, and if I knew how to manage it, I would go to him tonight."

The Old Man closed the book gently. "You see? What she's saying is, *if only; if only I had accepted him, faults and all; if only I had loved him while I could.*" He put the book back on the shelf. "That's when those sad words are the saddest of all: when it's too late to retrieve anything."

He stood up a bit stiffly. "Well, class dismissed. It has been good to see you, young man. Always is. Now, if you will help me find a taxi, I probably should be getting on home."

We came out of the building into the rainy night. I spotted a cruising cab and ran toward it, but another pedestrian was quicker.

"My, my," said the Old Man slyly. "If only we had come down ten seconds sooner, we'd have caught that cab, wouldn't we?"

I laughed and picked up the cue. "Next time I'll run faster."

"That's it!" cried the Old Man, pulling his absurd hat down around his ears. "That's it exactly!"

Another taxi slowed. I opened the door for him. He smiled and waved as it moved away. I never saw him again. A month later, he died of a sudden heart attack, in full stride, so to speak.

More than a year has passed since that rainy afternoon in Manhattan. But to this day, whenever I find myself thinking *if only*, I change it to *next time*. Then I wait for that almost-perceptible mental click. And when I hear it, I think of the Old Man.

A small fragment of immortality, to be sure. But it's the kind he would have wanted.

EPILOGUE

PRAYING THE SOLOMONIC PRAYER
Joseph Leininger Wheeler

Way back in the beginning years of our story ministry, letters from our readers began pouring in. Most were effusive, if not laudatory. More often than was good for me, writers would say, in so many words, *You are so wise!* Four words that represent the headiest of wine for writers young or old, famous or unknown, God-led or self-driven.

Pride represents the one enemy writers battle with most. Pride is such a protean force that it can come at you in so many forms that it is virtually impossible to identify its face. It is insidious. It is Luciferian—indeed, he was cast out of heaven because of it. Once pride gains the ascendancy, God Himself can no longer reach us. Scripture writers strongly imply that the so-called "unpardonable sin" is pride, because once pride mans our inner gates, God is walled out. And God refuses to invade our will.

Well, one never-to-be-forgotten day, in my mail was yet another of those insidious letters. My first response was pride-driven: *I must be one talented, brilliant guy!* But that morning, another Voice spoke up: "You are *not* wise. Only God is wise. Your ideas are not your own—they are His! You must weigh in on one side of the issue or the other: Either your ideas come from yourself—or they come from God. Now, *today*, you must decide."

In the soul-searching that followed, it didn't take me long to conclude that, without God, my ideas were worth no more than a pail of camel spit. And I was reminded of one of the most worthless books I've ever purchased. On the dust jacket, I was informed that, within the covers of this book, some of the world's leading authors would share their secrets about creativity, writing great books, wisdom, how to avoid writer's block, etc. What a farce! Instead, each and every one revealed how powerless they were to generate memorable writing on demand. Ideas would come on some days, and on other days they'd remain obstinately locked up. Significantly, not one of them made reference to God.

The upshot of all this was that my thoughts then turned to my own writing and editing. How could I personally become wise? More to the point: How could I get God to grant me wise thoughts and insights?

As I prayerfully mulled over my dilemma, thoughts of Solomon came to mind; according to Scripture, the wisest man who ever lived. I searched out the story and found it in 1 Kings 3:

That night the LORD appeared to Solomon in a dream, and God said, "What do you want? Ask, and I will give it to you!" . . .

"Now, O LORD my God, you have made me king instead of my father, David, but I am like a little child who doesn't know his way around. And here I am among your own chosen people, a nation so great and numerous they cannot be counted! Give me an understanding heart so that I can govern your people well and know the difference between right and wrong. For who by himself is able to govern this great nation of yours?"

The Lord was pleased that Solomon

had asked for wisdom. So God replied, "Because you have asked for wisdom in governing my people with justice and have not asked for a long life or wealth or the death of your enemies—I will give you what you asked for! I will give you a wise and understanding heart such as no one else has had or ever will have!" (1 Kings 3:5, 7–12, NLT).

And God followed through with his promise:

God gave Solomon very great wisdom and understanding, and knowledge as vast as the sands of the seashore. In fact, his wisdom exceeded that of all the wise men of the East and the wise men of Egypt. . . . His fame spread throughout all the surrounding nations. He composed some 3,000 proverbs and wrote 1,005 songs. He could speak with authority about all kinds of plants, from the great cedar of Lebanon to the tiny hyssop that grows from cracks in a wall. He could also speak about animals, birds, small creatures, and fish. And kings from every nation sent their ambassadors to listen to the wisdom of Solomon (1 Kings 4:29, 30, 32–34, NLT).

I had read this biblical account before, but never before had God given me this insight:

Nowhere in Scripture is it said that God wouldn't grant such a request from anyone else. More specifically, to *me*. The very thought that the great God of our universe would condescend to partner with the least of His children boggled my mind. But not having Solomon's temerity, rather than asking for a lifetime supply of wisdom, I meekly asked for but one day's worth. And breakers of wisdom rushed in upon me.

From that day to this, almost every day I pray what I call my Solomonic Prayer: "Dear Lord, it's me again. I come to you because my wisdom wells are shallow, and the water is brackish. Would you be willing to grant me— just for today—access to Your wisdom wells? For only Your wells are deep and contain vibrant living water." And God has never once let me down. If there be anything enduring about any of our books, it is because they originate with Him rather than with me.

But There's a Price to Pay

Yes, there *is* a price to pay for this divine gift: I am not at liberty to compartmentalize my life. I cannot write spiritually based books for one audience, then turn around and write books God would not condone or bless. Indeed, in God's sight, that is impossible: for everything we write or say or think is all part of one continuous bolt of cloth. Actually, it's easier to conceptualize now than it was in precomputer days. Reason why? Today you can Google any sentence or paragraph and find out, within reason, who wrote it. Teachers regularly use this to ascertain whether a given student plagiarized or not. If the quote comes from a published source, chances are it will be retrievable. In other words, you can no longer hide what you write!

Praying the Solomonic Prayer each day does something else: by constantly reinforcing my conviction that all real wisdom comes from God, it automatically takes self off the table. I can no longer take credit for God's insights. Whenever people compliment me on such things as how many of our books have sold, I now always qualify my response—such as, "Whatever success our books have had is a God-thing, not a Joe Wheeler-thing."

The result of this dramatic inner shift is that I no longer accept credit for anything—it is all *His*, not mine.

And more and more I have been passing on the good news to others that *anyone* can pray the Solomonic Prayer. No matter what one's profession may be, we may safely assume we can humbly ask God to grant us, each day (*always subject to His will*), access to His divine storehouses of wisdom—and He will grant such prayers. The only exceptions being if He would not bless certain questionable professions or involvements, or if we are taking credit for such wisdom rather than ascribing it to God.

Finally, let me say that every day with God at your side *is* an exciting day!

ACKNOWLEDGMENTS

"Introduction: The Diverging Roads of Our Lives," by Joseph Leininger Wheeler. Copyright © 2016. Printed by permission of the author.

PROLOGUE

"A Voice for God," by Jerome Hines, originally appeared in *Guideposts*, March 1963 and is reproduced with permission from *Guideposts*. Copyright © 1963. All rights reserved.

SECTION ONE

"The Golden Moment," author unknown. Published in *Their Word of Honor and Other Stories* (Takoma Park, MD: Review and Herald® Publishing Association, 1940). Reprinted by permission of Review and Herald® Publishing Association, Silver Spring, MD.

"Absent With Leave," Frederick Hall. Published in *The Youth's Instructor*, January 20, 1931. Reprinted by permission of Review and Herald® Publishing, Silver Spring, MD. If anyone can provide information about the author or the author's next of kin, please send it to Joe Wheeler (PO Box 1246, Conifer, CO 80433).

"Scars of Triumph," by Barbara Bradford. Published in *The Youth's Instructor*, January 30, 1962. Reprinted by permission of Review and Herald® Publishing, Silver Spring, MD. If anyone can provide information about the author or the author's next of kin, please send it to Joe Wheeler (PO Box 1246, Conifer, CO 80433).

"On the Far Side of Failure," by Arthur Gordon. Reprinted by permission of the Estate of Pamela Gordon.

"The Stranger Within Thy Gates," author unknown. If anyone knows the author or the original source of this old story, please contact Joe Wheeler (PO Box 1246, Conifer, CO 80433).

"Out of Focus," author unknown. If anyone knows the author or the original source of this old story, please contact Joe Wheeler (PO Box 1246, Conifer, CO 80433).

SECTION TWO

"To Bleed Awhile . . . and Fight Again," by Joseph Leininger Wheeler. Copyright © 2016. Printed by permission of the author.

"A Temperamental Garden," by Faith Harris Leech. Published in *The Youth's Instructor,* July 9, 1918. Reprinted by permission of Review and Herald® Publishing Association, Silver Spring, MD.

"Something to Carry Home," author unknown. Published in *The Christian Statesman,* n.d. If anyone can provide information about the author or the original publishing source, please send it to Joe Wheeler, (PO Box 1246, Conifer, CO 80433).

"Two Kinds of Tragedy," author unknown. Published in *The Youth's Instructor,* April 18, 1911. Reprinted by permission of Review and Herald® Publishing Association, Silver Spring, MD.

"When Success Hung in the Balance," by "A Father." Published in *The Youth's Instructor,* June 26, 1917.

Reprinted by permission of Review and Herald® Publishing Association, Silver Spring, MD.

"Polly Hastings' Valentine," author unknown. Published in *The Youth's Instructor,* January 29, 1929. Printed by permission of Review and Herald® Publishing Association, Silver Spring, MD. If anyone can provide information about the author or the author's next of kin, please send it to Joe Wheeler (PO Box 1246, Conifer, CO 80433).

SECTION THREE

"The First Settler's Story," by Will Carleton. Published in Carleton's book, *Farm Festivals* (New York: Harper & Brothers, 1881). Original text in the library of Joe Wheeler.

"The Girl Who Conquered Herself," by Margaret Sangster. Published in *The Christian Herald,* n.d. Reprinted by permission of *Christian Herald.*

"A Chance Encounter," by May Oakley. Published in *The Youth's Instructor,* October 18, 1927. Reprinted by permission of Review and Herald® Publishing Association, Silver Spring, MD. If anyone can provide information about the author or the author's next of kin, please send it to Joe Wheeler (PO Box 1246, Conifer, CO 80433).

"What One Lie Did," author unknown. Published in *The Youth's Instructor,* February 28, 1928. Reprinted by permission of Review and Herald® Publishing Association, Silver Spring, MD. If anyone can provide information about the author or the author's next of kin, please send it to Joe Wheeler (PO Box 1246, Conifer, CO 80433).

"He's Going to Die Anyway," by Harley Larkin. Copyright © 2015. Published by permission of the author.

SECTION FOUR

"The Countess and the Impossible," author unknown. If anyone can provide information about the author and publishing origins of this story, please send it to Joe Wheeler (PO Box 1246, Conifer, CO 80433).

"Tit for Tat," author unknown. If anyone can provide information about the author and publishing origins of this story, please send it to Joe Wheeler (PO Box 1246, Conifer, CO 80433).

"Poor Uncle Si," author unknown. Published in *The Youth's Instructor,* March 27, 1928. Reprinted by permission of Review and Herald® Publishing Association, Silver Spring, MD. If anyone can provide information about the author or the author's next of kin, please send it to Joe Wheeler (PO Box 1246, Conifer, CO 80433).

"Quiet Zone," by Alma Mager Campbell. Published in *The Youth's Instructor,* December 7, 1954. Reprinted by permission of Review and Herald® Publishing Association, Silver Spring, MD. If anyone can provide information about the author or the author's next of kin, please send it to Joe Wheeler (PO Box 1246, Conifer, CO 80433).

"Elnathan's Gold," author unknown. Published in *The Wellspring* and in *The Youth's Instructor,* January 26, February 2, 1926. Reprinted by permission of Review and Herald® Publishing Association, Silver Spring, MD. If anyone can provide information about the author or the author's next of kin, please send it to Joe Wheeler (PO Box 1246, Conifer, CO 80433).

"The Roadblock of Regret," by Arthur Gordon. Published in Gordon's book, *A Touch of Wonder*. Reprinted by permission of the Estate of Pamela Gordon.

EPILOGUE

"Praying the Solomonic Prayer," by Joseph Leininger Wheeler. Copyright © 2016. Printed by permission of the author.